Advance Praise for *Set Boundaries, Find Peace*

"This is the boundary bible. Nedra teaches us not only how to set healthy boundaries but to be clear about our feelings and intentions. Finding peace requires showing up—Nedra has written the blueprint on how to not only show up but also do the work."

—Alexandra Elle, author of *After the Rain*

"If you want the most comprehensive, relevant, and relatable guide to setting boundaries, speaking your needs, and living a more peaceful life, Nedra Tawwab's book on boundaries is for you."

—Sheleana Aiyana, author and founder of *Rising Woman*

"The book on boundaries we've all been waiting for! Nedra Tawwab offers clarity and direction with grace and compassion on a topic often discussed but rarely integrated. If you're ready to live in alignment and shift your relationship with self and others, *Set Boundaries, Find Peace* is your next must-read."

—Vienna Pharaon, LMFT, founder of Mindful Marriage & Family Therapy

"*Set Boundaries, Find Peace* breaks down the what, why, and how of boundaries in a clear and compassionate way, leaving you confident, empowered, and prepared to tackle those tough conversations."

—Melissa Urban, cofounder and CEO of Whole30

"Without healthy boundaries, we aren't able to fully live the life we want to live. This empowering book provides a powerful road map for establishing expectations and personal limits so that you can live your life with the safety, respect, and self-actualization that you deserve."

—Scott Barry Kaufman, PhD, host of *The Psychology Podcast* and author of *Transcend*

"*Set Boundaries, Find Peace* is a down-to-earth and practical guide on fully realizing your potential and giving yourself the freedom you deserve by clearly setting healthy boundaries in your personal and professional life, friendships, and relationships. Eye-opening and thoroughly engaging."

—Myleik Teele, CURLBOX founder

"A comprehensive guide on how to understand and establish interpersonal boundaries . . . Readers who follow Tawwab on social media and those who find setting boundaries especially difficult will appreciate the advice."

—*Publishers Weekly*

Set Boundaries,
Find Peace

Set Boundaries, Find Peace

| *A Guide to Reclaiming Yourself* |

NEDRA GLOVER TAWWAB

PIATKUS

PIATKUS

First published in the United States in 2021 by TarcherPerigee
First published in Great Britain in 2021 by Piatkus

18

A CIP catalogue record for this book
is available from the British Library.

ISBN: 978-0-349-42695-2

Book design by Silverglass
Printed and bound in Great Britain by
Clays Ltd, Elcograf S.p.A.

Papers used by Piatkus are from well-managed forests
and other responsible sources.

Piatkus
An imprint of
Little, Brown Book Group
Carmelite House
50 Victoria Embankment
London EC4Y 0DZ

An Hachette UK Company
www.hachette.co.uk

www.littlebrown.co.uk

Having healthy boundaries has changed my life in ways that I didn't know were possible. This book is dedicated to those of us who are gaining freedom through unapologetic, healthy boundaries.

Contents

Part 2
This Is How You Do the Work of Setting Boundaries

Preface

My life before I had healthy boundaries was overwhelming and chaotic. I, too, have struggled with codependency, peace in life and at work, and unfulfilling relationships. But setting expectations for myself and others gives me peace. Inventing a life with healthy relationships is an ongoing practice, but it gets more comfortable with time and practice.

The moment that I let up on setting perimeters, my old problems resurface. Because of this, I've made healthy boundaries a part of my life practice. Consistently, I am practicing assertiveness and self-discipline to create the life that I want. In the past, I carried around a lot of resentment, hoping that others would guess my mood and wishes. Through trial and error, I've learned that people will not guess my needs. They went about their day while I suffered in silence.

The things that I once found hard to say, such as "I won't be able to help you move," now come out more firmly. I was scared, I didn't want to make anyone mad, and I didn't know the right words. I feared that standing up for myself would cost me my relationships. All the while, the personal cost was much higher.

When I first learned about boundaries, I was confused about how the concept applied to my life. "Boundaries" can be such a broad and intimidating term. This book will break down the many aspects of having healthy boundaries and offer insights into how we can honor the boundaries set by others. It took me years to not feel *as* guilty setting limits with others, because I didn't know that guilt was normal when you're doing something that you believe to be mean. This book will teach you how to manage the discomfort (guilt) that stops you from having the life that you want. Hopefully, it will give you the confidence and courage to create healthy boundaries in your own life.

Introduction

Boundaries will set you free.

I've been a therapist for fourteen years. People don't come to therapy knowing they have boundary issues. When they walk in the door, boundary issues are disguised as issues with self-care, conflicts with other people, trouble with time management, or concerns about how social media impacts their emotional state.

Once they finish their tales of resentment, unhappiness, feeling overwhelmed, and codependency, I say to them gently, "You have an issue with boundaries." With that, we begin the work of uncovering boundary violations, learning to communicate boundaries to others, and dealing with the aftermath of setting boundaries. Yes, there's aftermath when dealing with the discomfort and guilt that comes from asserting yourself.

Instagram has become a space for me to post a lot of what I see as a result of boundary issues. My Instagram post "Signs That You Need Boundaries" went viral.

Signs That You Need Boundaries
- You feel overwhelmed.
- You feel resentment toward people for asking for your help.

- You avoid phone calls and interactions with people you think might ask for something.
- You make comments about helping people and getting nothing in return.
- You feel burned out.
- You frequently daydream about dropping everything and disappearing.
- You have no time for yourself.

The overwhelming response I see to these posts online shows me how much people relate to the need for boundaries. My direct messages overflow with notes like "Boundary issue, please help!" Weekly, I host Instagram Q&As, and 85 percent of the questions pertain to boundaries.

I receive questions like

"My friends get drunk every week, and it makes me uncomfortable when I hang out with them. What can I do?"
"I can't stop saying yes to my brother, who constantly asks to borrow money."
"My parents want me to come home for the holidays. I want to go to my partner's family's house instead. How do I tell them?"

Answering all the questions I get on Instagram is impossible. Week after week, people have more questions about their struggles with communication in relationships. I've uncovered a bottomless pit of boundary issues! I knew that the only way to help more people sort through these problems was to compile the strategies I've learned into a book. And these don't come just from my online and client work—I've had my own troubles with boundaries nearly my entire life. I continue to work on this every day, so I personally understand the deep importance of establishing healthy limits.

On most days, I ask a poll question on my Instagram Stories. Taking polls has been a fun way to learn from my community. At times I'm shocked by the results. Like the time I asked, "Are your expectations of your father different from the expectations you have for your mother?" Over 60 percent of people said no. I was shocked, because moms (I'm one) talk about expectations weighing more heavily on mothers. But the people of Instagram seemed to believe that both parents are equally as important. Sprinkled throughout this book you'll find my Instagram polls and results.

Like most people, I have found that my family relationships have been the most challenging for me in which to set boundaries. Family systems have unspoken rules of engagement. If you want to feel guilty, set a limit with your family.

Last year, I received a text from a relative calling on me to help them fix someone. I knew I'd grown when I wrote back, "This is not my job. And it's not your job either." After many years of trying to save the same person, I quit. It's not my job to save people. It's not my job to fix people. I can help people, but I can't fix them. At that moment, I was proud of my boundaries and how far I've come in my ability to honor them. Through trial and error, I've learned, "If you don't like something, do something about it." I had assumed that I had to accept things and help people, even if it harmed me. I did not want to disappoint others. This reflects the number one reason that people avoid setting boundaries: fear of someone getting mad at them.

Fear is not rooted in fact. Fear is rooted in negative thoughts and the story lines in our heads. Over the years, I learned that when people need my help, they have to recognize

Fear is not rooted in fact.

the issue and request assistance. And I have to be able and willing to help them. It took years for me to realize that I wasn't helping people by "fixing" them. I was getting in the way of them doing the work that they needed to do for themselves.

Throughout this book, you will learn about more of my boundary fails and triumphs.

It isn't easy to set limits, especially with the people we love. It may seem far worse to risk making someone mad than to have an uncomfortable conversation. But oh, the relationships *Clarity saves* I could have saved if only I had said something! *relationships.* Sometimes those things were big: "I will not be around you when you're drinking." And sometimes small: "Please take your shoes off when you come in my house." But they all mattered.

People don't know what you want. It's your job to make it clear. Clarity saves relationships.

This book presents a clearly outlined formula for knowing when you have a boundary issue, communicating the need for a boundary, and following it up with action. This process isn't always pretty. Communicating what you want and need is tough at first. And dealing with what comes after can be downright uncomfortable. But the more you do it, the easier it gets—especially when you experience the peace of mind that follows.

Reasons People Don't Respect Your Boundaries
- You don't take yourself seriously.
- You don't hold people accountable.
- You apologize for setting boundaries.
- You allow too much flexibility.
- You speak in uncertain terms.
- You haven't verbalized your boundaries (they're all in your head).

- You assume that stating your boundaries once is enough.
- You assume that people will figure out what you want and need based on how you act when they violate a boundary.

For fourteen years, I've been honored to help people make sense of their relationships and find the courage to create healthy relationships. In these pages, you will read stories to help you curate a deeper understanding of how boundary issues appear in real life. They are fictionalized versions of my interactions with clients. All names, identifying facts, and details have been changed to maintain anonymity. I hope you find yourself in these stories of others and learn how to shift your relationships.

Sometimes we know we need to set boundaries, but we have no clue how or where to start. This book serves as a guide to the benefits of limits and the hard work of setting expectations as you maintain your values in your relationships. Because we often don't know exactly how to express what we need, I've included wording suggestions. Feel free to use mine or practice your own phrases. Each chapter offers reflection questions or exercises to help you develop a deeper understanding of the material.

※

PART 1

Understanding the Importance of Boundaries

1

What the Heck Are Boundaries?

Boundaries are the gateway to healthy relationships.

"I feel overwhelmed," Kim said, burying her head in her hands. She had started seeing me two weeks after she had returned from her honeymoon. Newly married and excelling in her career, Kim prided herself on being the best at everything she did, but her worries about *getting it all done* had become all-consuming. She was depleted and dreaded getting out of bed in the morning. She not only was determined to be the best for herself, but she also always showed up as the "best" for others: the best friend, best daughter, best sister, best coworker. Now she wanted to be the best wife. And someday, the best mother. Being the best for Kim meant always saying yes. Saying no was mean. Saying no was selfish. She came to me hoping to figure out how to do more without feeling so exhausted.

On my couch, Kim went down the list of things she had agreed to do for other people in the coming week. She insisted that her friend *needed* her help to move. Her coworker would not be able to manage *his project* without her assistance. Kim was eager for solutions. She was trying to create more time to do all the things she'd signed up for.

As she rattled off everything she was trying to figure out, I asked her to pause. I gently pointed out that it was impossible to create more time. She looked a bit stunned at first. "Don't worry," I said. "I can help you lighten your load instead." From the look on her face, it seemed as though this approach had never occurred to her. I wasn't surprised. I meet so many people—especially women—who give and give so much, only to feel exhausted and even depressed as a result. This is why we live in a culture of burnout.

To start, I encouraged Kim to make a list of everything she needed to do at work and home that week. She already had her week completely mapped out (of course she did). She sketched a schedule for completing each task. She quickly saw that there was simply not enough time to do all the things she had planned.

I asked her, "What do you *really* have to do, and what can you delegate? Do you think your friend might be able to find someone else to help them move?" She mulled it over and said yes, but insisted that she *wanted* to help. At that moment, I could see that Kim had an issue with setting boundaries around how much and how often she's willing to help others and that this was contributing to her anxiety. She meant well, right? All she wanted to do was help people! But her level of willingness to help was impossible to sustain. She desperately needed to do *less*. When I mentioned delegating, Kim dismissed the idea immediately. She knew only one way to help others, and that was to say yes to doing it herself.

Kim's refusal to *say no* had led her to my office and was the root of her worry, stress, and crippling anxiety. According to studies, anxiety is rising. Complicated relationships are among the leading causes of increasing rates of anxiety, and anxiety and depression are the two most common reasons people pursue therapy. Just like Kim, people enter therapy when anxiety is starting to impact their daily life.

I worked with Kim to unpack her need to be present for everyone. I helped her see that saying no would give her the time she was seeking. Saying no would give her the freedom to settle into her role as a wife. Saying no would reduce her worry so that she could get out of bed and face the day without immediately feeling overwhelmed.

My Definition of "Boundaries"

Boundaries are expectations and needs that help you feel safe and comfortable in your relationships. Expectations in relationships help you stay mentally and emotionally well. Learning when to say no and when to say yes is also an essential part of feeling comfortable when interacting with others.

Signs That You Need Healthier Boundaries

Kim's ability to function was impacted by her constantly replaying her thoughts, planning, worrying about having enough time, and dreading getting started. In short, she was stressed out.

Mental health issues such as anxiety can be prompted by our neurological response to stress. When we are stressed, our brain has difficulty shutting down. Our sleep is affected. Dread sets in. As a therapist, I observe poor self-care, feelings of being overwhelmed, resentment, avoidance, and other mental health issues as common presentations of boundary issues.

Neglecting Self-Care

We've all heard the analogy from airplane-safety language: "Put on your oxygen mask *first* before helping others." Simple, right? Nope. *Neglecting self-care* is the first thing to happen when we get caught up in our desire to help others.

I can't tell you how many people show up in my office lamenting, "I don't have time to do anything for myself." After a quick evaluation, it becomes apparent that these people are not making *any* time for themselves. In fact, it often seems like they've forgotten how to take care of themselves. They can't manage to carve out time to eat a healthy meal or find five minutes to meditate, but they spend hours volunteering at their kids' school every week. This type of imbalance is an immediate sign of boundary issues.

Self-care is more than taking a spa day, and it isn't selfish. Saying no to helping is an act of self-care. Paying attention to your needs is self-care. And like putting on the ox-

The root of self-care is setting boundaries.

ygen mask, you'll have more energy for others if you apply it to yourself first. If you think about it, the root of self-care is setting boundaries: it's saying no to something in order to say yes to your own emotional, physical, and mental well-being.

Overwhelmed

Kim sought therapy because she was feeling chronically *overwhelmed*. This is one of the most common manifestations of boundary issues. Overwhelmed people have more to do than the time required for their tasks. They are drowning in thoughts about squeezing more into an already packed schedule. This type of busyness is endemic in our culture. Everyone is striving to do more and more. Time is an afterthought. But our well-being is the price. Understanding boundaries is a proactive way to gauge what is truly manageable, and it also allows you to give 100 percent to the task at hand without that nagging sense of *feeling overwhelmed all the time.*

Resentment

Feeling taken advantage of, frustrated, irritated, annoyed, and bitter is the result of the *resentment* we feel when we don't set limits. Being resentful impacts the way we deal with people. It doesn't allow us to be our best selves in our relationships. It breeds conflict. It makes us paranoid. It puts up a wall. Long-term resentment affects how we perceive the intentions of others. When we're resentful, we do things out of obligation to others instead of for the joy of helping. Resentment can be palpable.

If a client comes in and says, "I have to take care of my mother, and I feel angry about it," I can immediately pick up on the irritation and resentment. Exploring why they perceive pressure and obligation to provide this care allows me to challenge my client's belief. Yes, they want their mother to be taken care of, but they don't have to be the only person providing that care. Implementing boundaries—through asking for support from other family members and delegating—can help alleviate stress.

Remember the signs that you need boundaries:
- You feel overwhelmed.
- You feel resentful toward people for asking for your help.
- You avoid phone calls and interactions with people who might ask for something.
- You make comments about helping people and getting nothing in return.
- You feel burned out.
- You frequently daydream about dropping everything and disappearing.
- You have no time for yourself.

Avoidance

Disappearing, ignoring, or cutting people off is *avoidance*. Not responding to a request, delaying setting the record straight, or failing to show up are ways that we avoid situations instead of dealing with them proactively. But prolonging issues by avoiding them means the same issues will reappear over and over again, following us from relationship to relationship.

Avoidance is a passive-aggressive way of expressing that you are tired of showing up. Hoping the problem will go away feels like the safest option, but avoidance is a fear-based response. Avoiding a discussion of our expectations doesn't prevent conflict. It prolongs the inevitable task of setting boundaries.

Thoughts of fleeing—"I wish I could drop everything and run away"—are a sign of extreme avoidance. Fantasies of spending your days alone, ignoring calls, or hiding means you are seeking avoidance as the ultimate answer. But creating boundaries is the only real-life solution.

Learning to be assertive about your limitations with others will help you eliminate these symptoms and manage bouts of depression and anxiety. A lack of understanding about boundaries breeds unhealthy habits. So let's break it down.

Understanding Boundaries

Creating healthy boundaries leads to feeling safe, loved, calm, and respected. They are an indication of how you allow people to show up for you and how you show up for others. But it doesn't stop there.

The Meaning of Boundaries

- They are a safeguard to overextending yourself.
- They are a self-care practice.
- They define roles in relationships.
- They communicate acceptable and unacceptable behaviors in relationships.
- They are parameters for knowing what to expect in relationships.
- They are a way that you ask people to show up by upholding your needs.
- They are a way to communicate your needs to others.
- They are a way to create healthy relationships.
- They are a way to create clarity.
- They are a way to feel safe.

A boundary is a cue to others about how to treat you. It can be explicit, such as saying "I'm about to share something that I'd like you to keep between just the two of us." Or implicit, such as having a basket for shoes and socks right by the front door for guests. As you set your own limits, it's important to remain aware of the boundaries people are trying to communicate to you as well.

Our family histories and personalities determine how we implement and accept boundaries. If your family operates on unspoken limits or regularly ignores limits, you will probably grow up lacking the communication skills necessary to be assertive about your needs. For instance, adult children of alcoholics can have a difficult time setting limits. Parents with addiction issues often send the message that a child's boundaries are not more significant than the parent's addiction. So these children grow up struggling to understand and define limits. If your family of origin communicates and respects healthy limits, you are likely more comfortable defining them in any scenario.

Personality determines our comfort level with respecting and rejecting boundaries. People with anxious tendencies are more prone to overreact when challenged. Emotional regulation is a common issue, as these people are unable to react appropriately given the situation. People who exhibit strong signs of being disagreeable, such as always having to be right, arguing over small details, or struggling to accept differences in others, are more likely to push back against boundaries. Openness (receptiveness to change) and consciousness (willingness to learn and grow) are personality traits of people who are more likely to respect limitations.

Boundaries are essential at all stages. They change in relationships, just as the people in relationships change. Transitions such as getting married, going away to college, or starting a family often require new ones.

————

THERE ARE ACTUALLY three levels of boundaries. See if any of these sound familiar to you.

Porous

Porous boundaries are weak or poorly expressed and are unintentionally harmful. They lead to feeling depleted, overextending yourself, depression, anxiety, and unhealthy relationship dynamics. Kim from the opening story is an example of how porous boundaries can manifest and damage well-being.

Porous boundaries look like
- Oversharing
- Codependency
- Enmeshment (lacking emotional separation between you and another person)
- Inability to say no
- People-pleasing
- Dependency on feedback from others
- Paralyzing fear of being rejected
- Accepting mistreatment

———————————————— ❖ ————————————————

Examples of porous boundary setting:

- Saying yes to things you don't want to do
- Loaning money to people because you feel obligated or when you don't have the funds to do so

———————————————— ❖ ————————————————

Rigid

At the other extreme, rigid boundaries involve building walls to keep others out as a way to keep yourself safe. But staying safe by locking yourself in is unhealthy and leads to a whole other set of problems. Whereas porous boundaries lead to unhealthy closeness (enmeshment), rigid ones are a self-protective mechanism meant to build distance. This typically comes from a fear of vulnerability or a history of being taken advantage of. People with rigid boundaries do not allow exceptions to their stringent rules even when it would be healthy for them to do so. If a person with rigid boundaries says, "I never loan money to people," they never stray from that, even if a friend who isn't the type to borrow money is in a crisis.

Rigid boundaries look like
- Never sharing
- Building walls
- Avoiding vulnerability
- Cutting people out
- Having high expectations of others
- Enforcing strict rules

Examples of rigid boundary setting:

- Saying no harshly as a way to discourage people from asking you in the future
- Having a rule that you never watch your sister's kids

Healthy

Healthy boundaries are possible when your past doesn't show up in your present interactions. They require an awareness of your emotional, mental, and physical capacities, combined with clear communication.

Healthy boundaries look like
- Being clear about your values
- Listening to your own opinion
- Sharing with others appropriately
- Having a healthy vulnerability with people who've earned your trust
- Being comfortable saying no
- Being comfortable hearing no without taking it personally

Examples of healthy boundary setting:

- Saying no without apologizing because it's the healthiest choice for you at that moment
- Supporting people financially, when appropriate, and when you can do so without causing financial harm to yourself

---

Two Parts to Setting Boundaries

It's true that setting boundaries isn't easy. Paralyzing fear about how someone might respond can easily hold us back. You might play out awkward interactions in your mind and prepare yourself for the worst possible outcome. But trust me: short-term discomfort for a long-term healthy relationship is worth it every time!

Whenever you identify a boundary you'd like to set, remember that there are two steps to the process: communication and action.

Communication

Verbally communicating your needs is step one. People cannot accurately assume your boundaries based on your body language or unspoken expectations. When you explicitly state what you expect, there is little room for others to misinterpret what works for you. Assertive statements are the most effective way to do this.

Verbally communicating your boundaries sounds like this:

- "When we have a disagreement, I'd like you to use a lower tone and take a break if you feel like you're getting too heated in the argument. Also, I will mention when I'm becoming uncomfortable with your tone."
- "It's important to me that you honor plans that we set up. If you need to change our plans, please send me a text a few hours before."

Action

The process doesn't end with the communication. You must uphold what you communicate through your behavior. Betting on the other person to read your mind is a recipe for an unhealthy relationship. Action is required. For instance, let's say you've told your friend, "It's important to me that you honor plans that we set up. If you need to change our plans, please send me a text a few hours before." Because you've verbally communicated your boundary, when it's violated, you need to reinforce it with action. In this case, you would let your friend know that you can't accommodate the changed plans because they didn't give you enough notice. You might say gently, "I want to hang out with you, but my schedule won't allow for the adjustment. Let's set up a time to get together next week." It's hard, I know. But honoring your boundaries through action is the only way most people will understand that you're serious, which will help the people in your life become serious about your boundaries, too.

Boundaries Are for You and the Other Person

In my workshops, participants often share how they failed at communicating a boundary. Many people believe that once a limit is set, others will fall in line. Therefore, the person setting it doesn't take action after communicating it. But this lack of action invites continued violations in the relationship. You will have to put in the work to ensure that your boundaries are respected. It's your responsibility to follow through on it.

The biggest fear around this work is how others will respond, so let's get prepared for how that might look.

Common Ways People Respond When You Share Your Boundaries

It's important to consider how people might respond, but don't get too fixated on their possible reactions.

Common Responses to Boundaries
1. Pushback
2. Limit testing
3. Ignoring
4. Rationalizing and questioning
5. Defensiveness
6. Ghosting
7. Silent treatment
8. Acceptance

Pushback

It's typical for people to be resistant to changes in a relationship. It can be confusing at first. However, if someone respects you, they will respect these changes. We all grow and evolve, and our relationships must do the same. Pushback can happen at any time: immediately after you set a boundary or a while after, when the person decides to no longer honor it.

Pushback is a manifestation of the fear that things will be different, of being pushed out of the comfort zone. Even though "different" doesn't mean bad, some people will struggle to deal with new terms in the relationship.

Maybe after Kim tells her friend that she can't help her move, Kim's friend says, "Okay," as if she understands. Then the next day, Kim's friend says, "Are you sure you can't help me move? You're always the person who helps me."

Pushback sounds like

- "Well, I don't know if I can do that."
- "This isn't fair."
- "I have things I need, too, but I'm not making *you* change."

How to Handle Pushback

Acknowledge that you heard the other person's concern. Restate the boundary you initially set.

Examples:

"Thank you for letting me know. However, I'm proceeding with my request."

"I understand that you don't like my boundary, but I need to feel safe in my relationship. Having limits helps me feel safe."

Limit Testing

Kids do this a lot—it's part of forming independence when they are little—but adults do it, too. They heard you, but they want to see how much you're willing to bend. Let's say Kim tells her friend, "I can't help you move." Kim's friend then says, "Well, what about next week?" Her friend is trying to see if Kim has any flexibility. If Kim says, "Okay, next week," she is sending a clear message to her friend that the boundary is flexible.

Limit testing sounds like

- "I don't have to listen to you."
- "I'll check with you again to see if you can help."

How to Handle Limit Testing

Be clear about the behavior you notice. Name it: "You are testing my limits." Express how testing your boundaries makes you feel. "When you don't respect my boundaries, I feel ____." Then restate it. Explaining your boundary leaves room for people to object to your needs. In our attempts to make others feel comfortable, we might be persuaded out of setting healthy limits. Do your best to name your boundary without offering an explanation so that you aren't talked out of it.

Ignoring

People ignore boundaries as a passive-aggressive way of pretending they didn't hear them. But boundaries should be respected. When people ignore our requests, resentment builds. Over time, this erodes respect in the relationship.

Kim says, "I won't be able to help you move." Two days later, Kim's friend says, "When can you come to help me move this weekend?"

Kim has a few options here: restate her boundary, go with the flow by helping her friend, or not show up to assist with moving. Assertively, Kim could state, "I mentioned two days ago that I wouldn't be able to help you move." If she's too scared to restate her boundary, she'll likely end up helping her friend move, and her friend will likely ignore the next one Kim tries to set.

Ignoring boundaries looks like

- Doing what they want despite your boundary
- Acting as if your boundary was misunderstood

How to Handle Ignoring

Restate your boundary. Request that the other person repeat back what you stated. Stress the importance of the change moving forward. "I need this in future situations as well." React to ignoring immediately after you notice the issue. If not, the boundary will disappear.

Rationalizing and Questioning

Since you accepted behaviors in the past that you now deem inappropriate, people will react by asking questions as a way to rationalize their behavior as unproblematic.

In this scenario, Kim's friend responds with probing questions: "Why can't you help me move? I would help *you* move." Questions like these are hard to answer. It's tempting to start offering excuses or apologies. But it isn't helpful to say you're sorry about setting a boundary. Remember that people benefit from you *not* having limits. You have to look out for yourself—no excuses required. People may question your shift when you've done things that you are no longer willing to do. It's okay to let them know that you changed your mind or that the arrangement no longer works for you.

Rationalizing or questioning sounds like

- "Why are you asking me to change?"
- "What's the point of doing things differently now?"

How to Handle Rationalizing or Questioning
Be careful not to explain yourself. Keep your response short by saying something like "This is what's healthy for me." Saying too much will put you in a back-and-forth negotiation.

Defensiveness

This happens when people feel attacked. Being clear in our wording helps minimize defensiveness. However, some people will respond defensively no matter how you state your expectations and desires. Defensively, people will turn the issue on you because they don't want to be at fault.

In this situation, Kim's friend answers: "It's not like I move all the time, but fine if you don't want to help me." Defensive people aren't listening while you're talking; they're personalizing what you say and crafting a response. Their response has much more to do with them than it does with you. They are focused only on getting their needs met and resisting any change in your dynamic. But healthy relationships are not one-sided. The needs of both individuals are equally important.

Defensiveness looks like

- Turning your request around by making a request of you
- Explaining why they did something
- Accusing you of attacking them
- Bringing up what you've done in the past as a point of reference for your request

How to Talk to People When They're Being Defensive

- Make it about yourself, not them. Use "I" statements.
- Talk about one issue at a time.
- Don't talk about old issues with this person while stating your boundary.
- Use "feeling" words, such as "When you ____, I feel ____."
- Say something in the moment or soon after. Don't let issues fester for days, weeks, or months.
- Know your audience. If you can't talk in person, text or email your thoughts. Truly, some conversations are best had in person. But when you feel you won't be able to set the boundary face-to-face, set it by any means necessary.

Ghosting

Ending things without explanation or disappearing is often called "ghosting" and is an unhealthy response to boundaries. People who are passive-aggressive use this response. Rather than stating their objection, they try to show you how they feel through their actions. Ghosting happens right away or a few days after you have made your wishes known. It's generally a form of punishment.

For example, Kim says, "I won't be able to help you this weekend." Later that week, Kim texts her friend several times to check in or say hello, as she usually does, and her friend doesn't respond. Kim is sure that her friend is receiving the messages because she sees the read receipt marking them as read.

Ghosting looks like

- Not answering calls or texts
- Canceling plans

- Keeping in touch with mutual friends or contacts but leaving
  you out

How to Handle Ghosting

Send a precise text message or email mentioning the behavior you're noticing. People are likely to respond because they don't want to seem upset when they are. Express how the ghosting is making you feel and the concerns you have about the relationship. If receiving a response takes a few days, be clear to restate how the ghosting makes you feel. If you don't receive a response, remind yourself that their reaction was not about you. It was about their interpretation of the situation.

Silent Treatment

This response is less extreme than ghosting but still painful. It's also passive-aggressive and a form of punishing you for trying to set the boundary. This person will be noticeably distant after you assert your need. If you try to talk to them, they will offer short responses like yes or no. It's lonely and confusing to be the receiver of the silent treatment. The other person is present, but not really.

If Kim's friend used the silent treatment, it would go like this: Kim sees her friend the following week for a previously scheduled lunch date, and her friend isn't acting like her usual self. She's quiet and seems preoccupied. Kim tries engaging her friend in conversation, but her friend answers with one-word responses.

Silent treatment looks like

- Going hours/days without talking
- Providing short responses to questions to passive-aggressively express upset

---

How to Handle the Silent Treatment

Verbalize what you notice: "You seem upset. Can we talk about what I said to you?" Be clear about what you perceive to be the issue. Challenge the behavior of the other person. Perhaps offer feedback about why you set the boundary. "I was overwhelmed and unable to add another thing to an already full plate."

Acceptance

Acceptance is the healthy way to respond to boundaries and is a sign of a functional, mutual relationship.

In this case, Kim's friend says, "Thank you for letting me know." And just like that, Kim is off the hook for helping her friend move. No harm, no foul. Despite all the fear around boundary setting, in my experience most people will graciously accept your requests. When people respond in an unhealthy way, it's typically a sign that you needed limits a long time ago and that you need to reevaluate the relationship to assess whether your needs are being met satisfactorily.

Most likely, you've been denying the issues for far too long. Perhaps your issue is being asked to do things, saying yes, and resenting the other person for asking. Or your issue might be allowing someone to say things to you that make you uncomfortable.

Boundaries are the cure to most relationship problems. But both parties have to participate and respect the boundaries on either side.

Boundaries are the cure.

Signs of an Unhealthy Relationship

- You are unable to express your needs because the other person refuses to listen.
- The other person refuses to meet reasonable requests.
- There's emotional, physical, or sexual abuse.

- You feel sad, angry, drained, or disappointed after most interactions.
- The relationship is one-sided; you give and they take.
- There's a lack of trust in the relationship.
- The other person refuses to change some unhealthy behaviors.
- The other person has an addiction that is harmful to you.

———————————————— ❁ ————————————————

Boundaries grow and expand over time as our needs change.

Areas Where We Commonly Need Boundaries

Once you learn to identify boundary issues, communicate your needs, and follow up with action, you can start implementing boundaries in various aspects of your life. They are valuable in so many different scenarios. Here are the top areas where people struggle. We'll explore each of these in detail in the second half of the book.

Family

This will not come as a surprise to you: family is where people experience the biggest challenges around boundaries, especially within parent-child relationships. Adults are confused about how to navigate interactions with their aging parents. But parents should respect the limits and needs of their children, even when they are young. It's okay for a small child to set limits like not eating meat or feeling uncomfortable around certain people. Parents who respect those boundaries make space for their children to feel safe and loved, and they reinforce the positive habit of articulating needs. When parents ignore these preferences, children feel lonely, neglected, and like their needs don't matter—and they will likely struggle with boundaries as adults.

Siblings can also struggle with boundaries as they grow up. The older sibling may be used to operating in a particular manner, such as looking after younger siblings. But this role may not be needed after the younger sibling reaches a certain age. Dynamics in parent-child and sibling relationships get further complicated when spouses, grandchildren, and in-laws come into the mix. We will take a deep dive into the family system in Chapter 10.

Work

I see far too many people in my practice who are working way beyond the forty-hour workweek. They come in exhausted and frustrated, feeling powerless. But overwork is often more within your control than you think. It comes from having porous boundaries with your boss, your team, and your time. Limits can help you maintain a healthy work-life harmony. When you're unable to leave work at the office, disconnect on vacation, or shut off from work at a certain hour, you ignore your own boundaries at the expense of your well-being and often the well-being of your family. In Chapter 13, we'll take a closer look at identifying and resolving these issues in the workplace.

Romance

Boundary issues in dating relationships often arise when you oversell and underdeliver. This usually looks like agreeing to things in the beginning and not being able to keep up the pace as time goes on. Then, ultimately, you underdeliver on your promises. If you are shifting the way you're able to show up, verbalize what's causing the change. Be clear, such as saying something like "I won't be able to text frequently during the workday anymore because I have a new boss, and I want to make a good impression."

Boundary issues also come from putting way too many unspoken expectations on the other person. When it comes to love, for some reason we all want our partner to read our minds and know everything we want without having to ask. But this is an impossible expectation!

Being honest and up front (from the beginning, if possible) about what you expect and what you can offer will save you and your partner lots of heartache and arguments. In a long-term relationship, you'll have to set boundaries as each of you grows and the relationship evolves. This is especially true during transitions like moving in together, getting married, and having children. The good news is that whether expressed in the beginning or after years of being together, boundaries can connect the two of you in a new way and create space for open and assertive communication. We'll get to romance in Chapter 11.

Friendships

Toxic friendships—we've all had them. One day you look around and think, "Why am I even friends with this person? They consistently ____." (Fill in the blank: "let me down," "demand too much from me," "make me feel guilty," "flake on plans," and on and on.) Unhealthy friendships happen as a result of unhealthy boundaries. Friendships where you feel like you're giving more than you're receiving are harmful. Interactions with friends that often end in arguments are harmful.

Friends are your chosen family, and these relationships should bring ease, comfort, support, and fun to your life—not excess drama. In Chapter 12, I'll define a healthy versus an unhealthy friendship and take a look at what's holding you back from having healthy friendships. We'll also explore how to change or navigate out of a toxic friendship.

Technology

Adults and teenagers are reporting higher levels of anxiety and depression due to a fear of missing out (FOMO) and comparison games that arise from social media consumption. Infidelity is on the rise due to inappropriate usage of apps and social media. Technology brings new interpersonal challenges to the human experience—and it isn't going anywhere.

Technology will continue to advance at a rapid rate, so it's necessary to have limits in place to help you protect your happiness and relationships in the face of this pace. You need to determine how you will expand your boundaries to include technology in your life. Setting limits with devices is crucial within relationships and the family system, especially when it comes to children. In Chapter 14, we'll look further into technology boundaries.

Kim's issues were with saying no, but there are so many other ways that boundaries can help us.

Exercise

Grab your journal or a separate sheet of paper to complete the following exercise.

* Think of a time when someone said no to you. How did you react? Could you have reacted in a healthier way?
* Think of a time when you wanted to say no but didn't. How could you have expressed the boundary?
* How do you think people in your life will respond to your boundaries? Is this based on fact or your own assumptions? What about your past makes you think this?
* Where are you in need of boundaries right now? List three places or relationships where you would like to set a new one.

For more insight, take the Self-Assessment Quiz on page 255 to determine whether your boundaries are porous, rigid, or healthy.

2

The Cost of Not Having
Healthy Boundaries

Choosing discomfort over resentment.
—Brené Brown

Erica thought she had to be a hard worker, a great friend, and an all-around rock-star mom—all while looking like she slept eight hours a night. She worked forty hours a week as an accountant and was the single mother of two girls, ages seven and nine. When she wasn't at work, Erica was driving the girls around to activities. Her oldest played soccer, the youngest took dance classes, and both were active in the Girl Scouts, while also seeing tutors.

Her daughters' father provided only financial support and didn't help much with the kids. But Erica was still determined to give her girls the best life possible.

She based her perspective about motherhood on the fact that the other mothers around her seemed to be doing it all without any help. So after college, she didn't think anything of moving eight hundred miles away from her family.

This year, though, during her busy tax season, she started to unravel. The long days, nights, and expectations were becoming too much. Washing and putting the dishes away every night turned into dishes piled up in the sink. Her regular routine of washing a load of laundry per day turned into two weeks' worth of dirty laundry. She started zoning out while scrolling through social media on her phone, which made her late everywhere. The kids ate quick meals or frozen foods, as Erica paid no attention anymore to providing a balanced diet. Erica was unintentionally *on strike*.

At some point, she mentally said, "Screw it. How am I supposed to be a fantastic employee and mom at the same time?" She couldn't do it all, so she did as little as possible at home and spent almost no time with friends. When the girls tried to talk to her about the changes at home, she'd deny there was a problem. Then, for a few days, she'd get back into her old high-functioning rhythm of cleaning, cooking, and taking the kids to activities. But she couldn't stick with it, and would inevitably fall back into letting things go.

Erica started therapy at the urging of her friends, who saw her becoming burned out. While she was aware that she spent hours on social media and had become more withdrawn, she questioned whether she was actually experiencing burnout. After all, everything was fine at work. But she noted that work offered her support and praise, while the expectations were reasonable. At home, she said her job was thankless, never-ending, and mundane. She had no tools to advocate for herself at home like she did at work. There was no support system where she could vent her frustrations. She felt like she could never meet the expectations of being a *good* mother that she'd previously tried to achieve.

Erica had to create realistic expectations for her role as a mother, which meant setting healthy boundaries.

When I began seeing Erica, she spoke about her fantasies of running away and leaving everything. It wasn't that she didn't love her kids. Obviously, she did. It was just all so exhausting. She was frustrated with not being able to depend on their father. She resented having to ask him to pick up the girls from school or practices. Erica craved a well-balanced life for her daughters, but she was frustrated to be the only person responsible for making it work.

In my office, Erica told me she'd never heard her friends talk about motherhood in such a negative way. It made her feel ungrateful. And she'd always wanted to be a mom, so why wasn't she enjoying it? "The older the girls get, the more I pull away," she said. "At some point, I realized that motherhood would be endless." Giving Erica the space to talk openly allowed her to be honest about the feelings she'd been avoiding.

During one session, she had an aha moment when she realized her anger toward her ex-husband was being redirected toward her children. That emotional breakthrough led her to take small steps to be more focused at home. Instead of complaining about not having help, she hired a housekeeper to come in a few times a month. She asked her friends if they would be willing to watch the girls for a few hours while she spent time alone. She started giving the girls chores so that everything wouldn't be on her. Erica started managing burnout by letting go of the need to be a rock star and instead asking for help when she needed it.

What Can Happen When We Avoid Setting Boundaries
Burnout
Burnout is overwhelming, and boundaries are the cure. Burnout happens when people become emotionally, mentally, or physically exhausted. In many cases, like Erica's, it leads to chronic frustration, neglect in duties, moodiness, and avoidance. An article published by the *Harvard Gazette* found that doctor burnout costs the health care system $4.6 billion a year. As a result, doctors make critical medical mistakes, misdiagnosing illnesses, prescribing the wrong medications, and not paying attention to essential details.

According to Emily Nagoski and Amelia Nagoski, the authors of *Burnout: The Secret to Unlocking the Stress Cycle*, burnout is caused by stress, which they describe as "the neurological and physiological shift that happens in your body when you encounter [triggers]."

Burnout is caused by

- Not knowing when to say no
- Not knowing how to say no
- Prioritizing others over yourself
- People-pleasing
- Superhero syndrome ("I can do it all")
- Unrealistic expectations
- Not being appreciated for what you do

Let's go through each of these for Erica.

Not Knowing When to Say No

Despite knowing that her busy season at work was coming up, Erica made no preparations to do less. Instead, she wanted to continue to operate at the same pace as she had during her typical work season. She even added another activity to her kids' schedule at her busiest time of year.

Without additional support, Erica would have to

Get the kids and herself ready,
take them to school,
work 9:00 a.m. to 5:00 p.m.,
pick up the girls from school,
take them to activities,
prepare dinner,

clean the house,
help with homework,
get the girls ready for bed,
plug back in for work,
prepare for the next day, and
sleep five to six hours.

Then she had to start it all over the next day.

Suggested Boundaries

Most parents want their children to be well-rounded, but that doesn't have to come at the expense of the parents' sanity. Erica could check with other parents in her neighborhood to see if carpooling is an option. She could also lighten her load by saying no to anything beyond one activity per semester for her girls.

Not Knowing How to Say No

"No" is extremely difficult to say, especially when you want to do it all. Erica had to learn to be okay with not doing it all and also not allowing her daughters to get fixated on doing it all.

Suggested Boundary

Instead of saying yes to all extracurricular activities, Erica could wait a semester to see if the girls are still interested. Giving kids time helps them think through their options. The ability to try everything doesn't allow children to become good at any one activity.

Prioritizing Others Over Yourself

Erica's daily to-do list didn't include anything for relaxing or reconnecting to herself. Work, home, and kids were the focus of her days. *She* was completely missing from her list.

SUGGESTED BOUNDARY

Erica could schedule time for herself every day, engaging in a quick morning routine. For example:

- Do a wake-up stretch (two minutes).
- Meditate or sit quietly (two minutes).
- Read something inspirational (two minutes).
- Write down thoughts and one thing you're grateful for (two or three minutes).
- Recite a positive affirmation or intention for the day (one minute).

Repeating this plan before bed would also be helpful. Sticking to a morning and evening routine would ensure that Erica had time to connect with herself daily.

People-Pleasing

Erica had a lot of people she wanted to please—her children, boss, and friends. She wanted to be a better mother than her mother had been to her. In trying to please everyone, however, she was left with little energy to care for herself.

SUGGESTED BOUNDARY

I suggested that Erica start asking herself "Why is this important to me?" and do only what is most important. Sometimes we do things that aren't important to us but that we believe maintain a particular image of "good parent" or "person who has it all together."

Superhero Syndrome (I Can Do It All)

No one can do it all. Believing we can leads to burnout. In Erica's case, she saw the mom bloggers who posted gorgeous pictures of themselves holding their well-dressed babies. For a long time, she believed it was possible to do everything and still cook carefully plated meals every day. She had no perspective on the average woman's struggle to manage work, life, and relationships, even though she was living it herself.

SUGGESTED BOUNDARY

Stop following people on social media who make it appear they have it all together all the time. Connect more with mothers who are honest about the struggles of their everyday lives, and share ways to manage stress.

Unrealistic Expectations

Erica had been washing a load of laundry daily, cooking dinner, working, driving her kids around, and working some more. Her expectations weren't reasonable, realistic, or sustainable. I suggested she ask herself some questions: *Whose expectations am I fulfilling? Do my kids believe I'll say yes to every request? Does my family require one-hour recipes every night?* Then she considered that perhaps her expectations were unreasonable. Realistic expectations don't lead to stress.

SUGGESTED BOUNDARY

Erica had tasks on her plate that she didn't have to do herself. She became willing to ask for help or hire help so that she could do less and delegate more. We can't create more time, but we can do less, delegate, or ask for help.

Not Being Appreciated for What You Do

Erica's burnout didn't extend to work, because she received recognition for her efforts and felt valued there. This gave her the incentive to be great at her job. At home, however, Erica didn't receive any praise for her efforts.

SUGGESTED BOUNDARY

Tell people what you need. Erica has become aware that she needs positive feedback and affirmation. Communicating this need to her family could give her the push she needs.

HERE ARE A few additional issues that commonly lead to burnout:

Things That Lead to Burnout
- Listening to people complain about the same things over and over
- Doing your best with little appreciation for your work
- Dispensing your advice to people who don't value your feedback
- Engaging in dialogue with people who take an emotional toll on you
- Doing things that don't make you happy
- Lacking balance (harmony) in your roles and duties
- Setting high expectations at work, at home, or in relationships
- Having a continual urge to control situations outside of your control

Mental Health and Boundaries

Mental health issues are not the cause of an inability to say no, be assertive, and advocate for ourselves. But this inability can certainly be exacerbated by mental health problems. For example, ruminating, which is replaying thoughts over and over in our heads, is a behavior that comes with some diagnoses. Focusing on how others might respond is one way we ruminate, which impacts our ability to act. Boundary issues are more pronounced with the following mental health problems.

Anxiety

When people seek therapy, it's usually for anxiety and/or depression. According to the Anxiety and Depression Association of America, 40 million adult Americans have been diagnosed with anxiety and approximately 20 million with depression. Many people are diagnosed with both.

First, let's take a closer look at anxiety. It's often triggered by setting unrealistic expectations, the inability to say no, people-pleasing, and the inability to be assertive. When people come to me with anxiety, we begin to dissect the different aspects of their lives and to work on ways to minimize the triggers that cause them to become anxious.

Based on my experience with clients, the biggest trigger for anxiety is the inability to say no. So helping people with anxiety means assisting them in setting boundaries.

Saying no is the most obvious way to set one. But rather than appear mean or displease someone, we often agree to things we don't want. We may agree to do something that we don't have time to do or that we don't really know how to do.

Then we become anxious about all the things we've said yes to doing with and for others. We worry about getting it all done and doing it correctly. As these worries flood our brain, we experience anxiety. So setting a limit about what we're reasonably able (and willing) to do is one way to manage anxiety triggers.

Unrealistic expectations of yourself and others can also trigger anxiety. Sometimes, expectations arise as a result of comparing yourself with others, or your expectations may come from family or cultural norms or your friends. If you deal with frequent anxiety, it's important to become aware of what is a reasonable expectation and what isn't. To determine if your expectations are reasonable, consider this:

1. Whose standard am I trying to meet?
2. Do I have the time to commit to this?
3. What's the worst thing that could happen if I don't do this?
4. How can I honor my boundaries in this situation?

For people with chronic anxiety, the most challenging part of this process is the fear of what others might think. In an anxious state, people create scenarios that lead to adverse outcomes if they try to set a boundary. "If I say no, they'll say I'm being selfish and abandon me," for example.

Even though the worst case is the least likely outcome, when you're anxious, it's exactly what you work hard to avoid. But the true worst-case scenario is avoiding boundaries. Saying no to others allows you to say yes to yourself or to things you truly want.

Affirmations for people who struggle with anxiety:

"I'm entitled to have expectations."
"In healthy relationships, my desires will be acknowledged and accepted."
"After I set limits, people will remain in a relationship with me."
"I can set standards even through my discomfort."

Now let's take a look at how boundaries impact depression.

Depression

When I treat depression, I'm treating hopelessness. My work with depressed clients involves empowering them to believe in themselves. When they're able to do that, their lives get better. One of the ways I instill hope is by helping them set simple boundaries. They come up with something small and request that another person adhere to that little request. We start with baby steps.

For instance, I will say, "The next time you go out to eat and your order isn't prepared correctly, make a promise to yourself to ask for it to be corrected." Starting with a less daunting boundary with a stranger may seem trivial, but when people suffer from depression, they often find it hard to advocate for themselves in any situation. When this assignment is executed, my clients with depression can see how a request can be honored. From there, we start to work on more challenging requests.

Examples of Less Harmful Boundaries
- Accepting assistance to your car at the grocery store
- Correcting people when they say your name wrong
- Asking for help while shopping instead of trying to find merchandise on your own
- Asking questions instead of assuming you know the answer

If you experience depression, it can be helpful to set boundaries about how many things you expect yourself to do in a single day. If you add too much to your to-do list but lack the motivation, you'll set yourself up for failure. Depression will increase if you take on too much without finishing any of the tasks you started. Instead, highlight the small wins, such as showering over the weekend, going to the gym, or going out with friends.

Affirmations for people who struggle with depression:

"Little by little, I can keep small promises to myself."
"Small wins are big wins."
"Doing one thing is better than doing nothing at all."

Dependent Personality Disorder (DPD)
DPD is characterized by the inability to be alone. A person with DPD feels helpless without the assistance of another person, leaving no

room for boundaries in relationships. People with DPD continuously seek attention, advice, and comfort from others. Their reliance on others for decision-making and constant feedback often damages the relationships of people with DPD.

Borderline Personality Disorder (BPD)

People who experience BPD have unhealthy attachments in their relationships with others. Their relationships are usually unstable because they overpersonalize their interactions with others, making assumptions and overreacting. Those with BPD often lack boundaries, as they find it hard to differentiate where they begin and others end. The separation between them and other people is blurred.

ADDITIONALLY, PEOPLE STRUGGLING with substance use, psychotic disorders, and eating issues are likely to experience problems with boundaries.

Let's take a look at how these issues present in our relationships with ourselves and others.

What Relationships Without Boundaries Look Like

Carlos considered himself a good friend. When his roommate asked to borrow his car, he immediately said yes. He didn't ask any questions and trusted his roommate would do right by him.

When his roommate returned, however, Carlos immediately smelled cigarette smoke in the car and saw that the tank was nearly out of gas. "What kind of person smokes in another person's car and leaves the tank almost empty?" he thought. He was disappointed to find that his roommate failed to meet his unspoken expectations.

Communicating our boundaries isn't easy, but without it, we set ourselves up for long-term suffering. We simply can't have a healthy relationship with another person without communicating what's acceptable and unacceptable to us. If we aren't proactive about this in our relationships, we can be sure the other person will set *their* boundaries. That forces us to operate by their rules and their rules only.

In Chapter 6, I will show you how to communicate boundaries clearly, but know that if you haven't told

Boundaries are not unspoken *rules.*

someone what yours are, they can't possibly know. People can't meet a standard that we never express. Boundaries are not *unspoken* rules.

Unspoken boundaries are invisible, and they often sound like "They should've known better" or "Common sense would say . . ." Common sense is based on our own life experiences, however, and it isn't the same for everyone. That's why it's essential to communicate and not assume that people are aware of our expectations in relationships. We must inform others of our limits and take responsibility for upholding them.

Relationships that have the potential to be healthy often become unhealthy because of either rigid or porous boundaries. Either we are strict about them, or we give people free rein with no limits. These scenarios create one-sided relationships, in which one person does most of the work to keep the relationship going.

But healthy relationships are between two people who are mutually supportive of each other. (The only occasion when one-sided relationships are appropriate is in the parent-child dynamic.)

Simply put, relationships without boundaries are dysfunctional, unreasonable, and hard to manage. They operate mostly based on the assumption that something "magical" will happen to turn it all around. But hoping that our relationships will repair themselves out of nowhere is a long shot at best.

Without boundaries in relationships, we also can't have healthy self-care practices. In fact, most people without healthy limits think that engaging in self-care is selfish, so it feels terrible when they try to do it. They believe that their self-care is at the expense of being there for another person. Self-care brings up feelings of guilt, because they feel like others will fall apart without their help.

In these kinds of relationships, our role is that of a helper. We worry about the other person and don't trust that they can care for themselves unless we enable them. Our attention is multifocused because we are continually trying to balance the needs of multiple people with our own needs. Even when we try to focus on ourselves, we tend to still focus on others and base our decisions on what these other people might think.

Without boundaries, relationships usually end, or we become fed up from being mistreated. Sometimes we allow mistreatment for so long that we can't take it anymore. Then, since we never clearly communicated our unhappiness, the other person is shocked to find out how much we suffered.

When we do become clear about our expectations, saying "I need you to ____," we at least learn exactly who is and isn't willing to honor what we need and want.

In your relationships, are people clear about how you desire to be treated? How are you treating yourself? Others learn a lot about you from watching how you treat yourself. People can sense your lack of self-esteem or neediness based on how you talk to yourself, talk about yourself, and treat yourself behaviorally. Be kind to yourself, because the people in your life are watching. This doesn't mean that people have a right to be mean.

Common Feelings When We Don't Set Boundaries

When you say yes but want to say no, you feel something "off" in your body. When you allow people to take advantage of you, you feel something in your body that isn't right. When you give to others begrudgingly, you feel it in your body.

So if you learn to pay attention to your body, it will tell you when it's time to set boundaries—in the sigh before you answer your phone, the desire to avoid certain people, or your hesitance to say yes. You might also feel a tightness in your belly, an ache in your shoulder, or a pain in your neck or temple. As you become more aware of your personal signs, you'll discover how often you put your own needs aside to please or take care of others.

The emotions that people most commonly feel when they don't set boundaries are resentment, anger, and frustration. Here are a few common causes of these emotions in relationships:

- Feeling unheard
- Setting a boundary but not gaining the result you desired
- Committing to things you don't want to do
- Feeling used
- Avoiding setting boundaries

Let's break down each of these emotions in a bit more detail.

Resentment

At its core, resentment is disappointment. Then you mix in anger and fear. Because resentment is often an uncomfortable emotion to admit and express, many people deny feeling it. So they often express it in a passive-aggressive way. Instead of acknowledging "I'm feeling resentful," they hint at the feeling through terse and evasive conversation. Or they avoid time with the offending person or dismiss the impact of the offensive behavior. Instead, they assume the other person should just figure out why they're upset.

Anger

Anger is a feeling of hostility or annoyance, and it can be expressed inwardly or outwardly. When expressed inwardly, people with unhealthy boundaries engage in negative self-talk, self-sabotage, self-blaming, or low self-esteem. Instead of holding others accountable, the anger becomes an issue within. This often causes anxiety, depression, or other mental health issues.

Anger toward others looks like blaming without personal accountability, adult tantrums (yelling, cursing, rage, crying fits, breaking things, verbal abuse), or an overall apathetic disposition toward others.

Both inwardly and outwardly expressed anger can negatively impact relationships.

Frustration

Frustration ensues when we're unable to achieve a goal or get a need met—when we try something and feel that we failed. For example, let's say you work up the courage to set a boundary and communicate it to another person, only to find that they don't honor it. This is sure to cause frustration. When we feel frustrated after making our expectations known, we say things like "Well, they won't listen anyway" or "I already tried that, and it didn't work." Frustration leads to a loss of hope and motivation.

But feeling frustrated isn't a reason to stop trying to implement boundaries. Setting them takes perseverance. There are so many reasons why setting them might not have worked. Here are a few:

- The other person wasn't ready to hear you.
- What you said was misunderstood because you didn't follow through with the boundary you set.
- You failed to honor the boundaries you set up, so people couldn't understand that you were serious.

- You made a request but didn't set a boundary.

Whatever the reason, you can try again. Don't allow frustration to hold you back from getting your needs met.

Things We Do to Avoid Setting Boundaries
Move Away

"I just moved away so they would stop asking me to do things." I've heard this several times from clients in my office. It may seem like an easy fix to blame the other person and leave their physical proximity, but you will almost certainly find yourself creating new relationships with the same boundary issues. Besides, technology has made it easier for us to be tempted to offer long-distance support emotionally and financially. We can call, talk, and text without huge costs, and depending on where we move, the other person might be able to quickly visit. Distance doesn't always solve the problem, so a physical shift is simply not the answer. It's a mental change that's required. And then we change our behaviors to align with what we say we need.

The truth is that unhealthy boundaries will follow you wherever you go unless you learn to verbalize them.

Gossip

Here's the definition of "gossip":

- Talking about people in a judgmental manner with the intent to cause harm
- Making statements behind the back of the person being discussed

---

Instead of setting a direct boundary, we often use gossip as a way of processing our frustrations. But gossip isn't helpful and only leads to more resentment. It does nothing to improve the relationship or end the behavior that bothers us.

Complaints

Complaining to others won't fix our unhealthy boundaries. Similar to gossiping, complaining is another way of processing frustration. However, with complaining, we usually play the role of victim, saying things like "Why does everyone expect so much from me? My husband knows I need help, but he doesn't offer. I don't understand why people can't do things for themselves."

Along with not being a solution, complaining—much like gossiping—builds resentment. As we air our grievances, we become more frustrated and annoyed, reinforcing the belief that others are doing things *to* us. We don't stop to evaluate what we're *allowing* to happen by not setting clear boundaries.

Avoidance

When I bought a new car, I didn't want to tell people they couldn't borrow it. I thought making it difficult for them would end the issues with borrowing. But then they started asking me to drive them places. By not creating a boundary, I created a new problem.

There's nothing easy about these tough conversations. We don't want to hurt anyone's feelings, so we allow issues to fester. Then we inevitably become resentful, angry, or frustrated. We hope that eventually people will figure out what our avoidant behavior means and change of their own accord.

For example, while in college I lost interest in a guy I was dating. As he continued to call, I rarely answered, thinking he'd eventually get the point and stop calling. When I did answer, I used excuses like

"Between work and school, I don't have time to hang out" and "I have homework." The truth was, I simply didn't like him.

After a few weeks, I couldn't take it anymore. When he called, I said, "I don't like you in the same way you like me. I think you should stop calling." Guess what? Just like that, he stopped calling. I was no longer annoyed every time my phone rang, and he was free to call someone who was really interested in him. Everyone was happy.

Avoidance wasn't an effective strategy for me, and it isn't for you either. In the gentlest way possible, say "No, thanks, that doesn't work for me; I'm not interested." Or, "No, you can't borrow my car." Don't waste your time and anyone else's time hoping they will figure it out.

Cutoff

A cutoff is when you abruptly (sometimes without explanation) disconnect from another person. Before you cut people off, ask yourself this:

1. Was the other person aware of my issues with the relationship?
2. Have I tried setting a boundary?
3. Did I uphold my boundary and hold the other person accountable?

Cutoffs happen as a result of believing that the other person is incapable of change, that they won't honor our boundary, or that we have let things go so far that we're no longer interested in repairing the relationship. Cutting people off may seem like an easy way to resolve relationship issues, but we can't escape setting limits if we want healthy relationships.

Exercise

This chapter began with Erica's story about burnout. During a retreat, I learned an activity that I've shared with my clients, many of whom found it helpful. The "What's on Your Plate?" exercise is a constructive way to identify what you already have on your plate before committing to more.

On a separate sheet of paper, write down all of the duties, activities, and responsibilities attached to your various roles in life. Use the key below, and put a symbol next to each item. (Some may require more than one symbol.)

After you've completed the activity, ask yourself:

- Are you surprised by anything on your list?
- What's missing from your list?
- What do you have to eliminate to spend more time on the things you enjoy?

In the next chapter, we'll discuss why we tolerate boundary issues, why it's so hard to set limits, and how childhood trauma and neglect make this process uniquely challenging for us.

3

Why Don't We Have
Healthy Boundaries?

Boundaries are the key to healthier relationships.

"You are now the man of the house," Justin's mother said to him after his parents divorced. He was twelve years old. Suddenly feeling responsible for his younger brothers, Justin began watching them after school, started their dinners in the evening, and helped get them ready for bed. He even took them along when he hung out with his friends.

Justin's mother was absent a lot, both physically and emotionally. When she wasn't working, she was debilitated by depression in the wake of the divorce. His father had moved on and was dating a woman who had children of her own. So even though he was still a child himself, Justin became the caretaker and emotional support for his family.

His mother asked his opinion about how to take care of his brothers. She cried and shared her emotions about the divorce with him. Among his peers, Justin was considered "mature" for his age. They saw him as wise, so they quickly opened up to him.

When he came to me, Justin was twenty-nine years old, but he was still heavily involved in caring for his brothers. In fact, he was the go-to person for most of the people in his life. His friends leaned on him for sound advice, both his parents called him whenever there was an issue with his brothers, and his brothers used him for financial and emotional support. By twenty-nine, he was tired of always playing the role of the responsible problem solver, but he couldn't see a way out. After all, *everyone needed him.*

The pattern even affected Justin's romantic relationships. He always found the "project" person to date—someone who needed help. His longest relationship lasted nine months, but once his partner no longer needed him, the relationship quickly fizzled. He was aware that he tended to attract needy people. He didn't particularly enjoy helping others, but he did believe his help was necessary.

As he constantly gave to others, Justin never asked for help for himself. He was self-sufficient and self-reliant, and feeling helpless made him uncomfortable. Even when a girlfriend tried to do something nice for him, he didn't like it. He hoped to get married and have children. But maintaining attachments with anyone other than his existing family and friends was a challenge.

Justin needed to learn how to acknowledge his emotional needs and allow others to be there for him. During his parents' divorce, he came to the conclusion that his needs were too complicated for others and that he was better at *giving* support than *receiving* it. It was clear that his relationship issues were the product of the emotional neglect he'd experienced as a child.

Emotional neglect happens when you don't receive sufficient emotional support from a parent or caregiver. They may not understand a child's needs, or they may devalue the need to nurture a child's emotional well-being. People who are emotionally neglected are often confused about what they experienced. There's a difference between emotional abuse and emotional neglect, however. Emotional neglect is unintentional, while emotional abuse is more deliberate.

People who experienced emotional neglect tend to have issues developing healthy attachments to others, whether their attachment is anxious or avoidant.

We focused Justin's initial recovery on learning how to set emotional boundaries with his brothers and parents. At first, he felt uncomfortable saying to one of his brothers, "Have you asked Mom?" rather than jumping to solve a problem for them himself. He also felt it would be mean to speak to his mother about no longer being her emotional confidant.

But over time, Justin noticed how his family began to see him differently. He started to talk more about himself with them and with the women he dated. He began to trust that people wanted to know about him and what he was feeling. Eventually, he was able to date someone for more than a few months. He became a son to his parents again, rather than parenting them. It wasn't comfortable for him in the beginning, but Justin was gradually able to communicate and uphold his boundaries.

What's Keeping Us from Having Healthy Boundaries?

It's your responsibility to tell people how burdened you are in your relationships. Justin knew he wanted to step back from the caretaking role with his siblings. He was tired of being the emotional support for his parents, and he knew he had dating issues. But he didn't realize the solution to his problems could be setting boundaries in his relationships.

"It's Them, Not Me"

For our relationships to improve, we assume that the *other* person has to change. We're unaware of the aspects that are within our control, such as setting boundaries. But when we do set boundaries, our relationships change because we've changed what we're willing to tolerate.

"We Tried Once, and It Failed"

When we set a boundary and nothing changes immediately, we often assume it's a lost cause. But there are many reasons why people don't immediately adhere to our request, so the way we communicate it is critical. What we do after we've stated what we want is also vital. (You will learn the best ways to set and maintain boundaries as you continue reading.)

Misinterpreting What Boundaries Are

A common misconception about boundaries is that they always mean saying no. But we can set boundaries in many ways; saying no is just one of them. Justin set his by redirecting his brothers to talk to their parents about specific issues. He also set boundaries with himself about being more emotionally transparent in his interactions with others. Justin didn't exactly say no to his parents when they tried to use him as their emotional support. However, he was forthcoming that he felt uncomfortable hearing about certain topics. There's more to boundaries than saying no.

There's more to boundaries than saying no.

The Reasons We Tolerate Boundary Issues

We Aren't Aware That We Need to Set Boundaries

In Chapter 1, we discussed signs that we might need to set a boundary. The most significant symptom is *discomfort*, which manifests itself as anger, resentment, frustration, and burnout. When we feel any of these, we likely need to set a boundary.

We tolerate unhealthy boundaries because we don't understand our feelings, and we fail to notice the discomfort. We see that something is "off," but we're unaware of what is causing the discomfort.

The film *What's Eating Gilbert Grape?* is a great example of this. Gilbert (played by Johnny Depp) is a parentified teenager who cares for his younger siblings, one of whom is autistic (Arnie, played by Leonardo DiCaprio). Gilbert also cares for his mother, who is obese and housebound. Her weight gain began after her husband committed suicide.

Gilbert struggles to have a social life outside of his family because he has unhealthy boundaries. Two of his siblings manage to build their own lives—one becomes the manager of a bakery, and the other goes away to college. But when Gilbert starts a romance with a girl visiting his town, nothing comes of it because he doesn't create any boundaries with his family. While Gilbert is aware something is off, he isn't aware that healthier limits could help him start a life outside of the one he's known.

We Focus on the Worst-Case Scenario

Despite the fact that the worst-case scenario is often the least likely to occur, our fears of the worst tend to keep us from setting boundaries.

Here are some typical worst-case-scenario thoughts:

"What if they get mad at me?"
"What if they want nothing to do with me?"
"What if I lose a friend/family member?"
"What if I say the wrong thing?"
"Is setting a boundary petty?"
"What if I'm called selfish?"
"I don't think anyone will listen to me."

Worst-case-scenario thinking is fear-based, and it's the wrong hypothesis about what is most likely to happen. We can't predict the future. We can't predict how people will respond to our boundaries.

The only thing we're able to control is our own behavior. Our biggest fear is that we'll lose people, so we tolerate boundary issues to maintain our relationships.

We Feel We Can't Tolerate the Discomfort of Setting Boundaries

Setting limits is uncomfortable, and that discomfort is enough for most of us to shy away from setting them. So we stay silent. We can't tolerate the discomfort of having what we assume will be difficult conversations (worst-case-scenario thinking again). One of the things I teach people is how to manage the discomfort of setting boundaries. We may not feel comfortable having difficult conversations, but we can do it. The short-term discomfort of setting a boundary isn't a reason to continue tolerating the longer-term discomfort of the issues that inevitably result. Unhealthy relationships are frustrating and damaging to our long-term well-being. Over time and with consistent practice, setting boundaries becomes easier.

Where We Learn About Boundaries
Family Is Where It All Starts

We are born with the urge to have our needs met. That's why we cried, fussed, and acted out when we wanted something. We learned whether we could get our needs met based on how our parents and other caretakers responded. Parents/caregivers can guide us toward either healthy or unhealthy boundaries.

From birth, the family is our primary teacher. We first learn from our mother and father, then others in the home environment, including siblings and extended family. In many cases, when we think about boundaries in the family, we think about rules set by our parents. Boundaries are not necessarily rules, however. Limits that parents have with children are expectations, preferences, and sometimes rules. Parents and caregivers typically feel comfortable communicating their expectations to children. But children often feel they don't have a right to set boundaries for themselves.

Respecting Kids' Boundaries

When my oldest daughter was around four months old, she started to demonstrate disdain toward her caregiver at our local family gym. Generally, my daughter enjoyed being held, but she didn't like this one person in child care. Whenever we left her in child care, she would cry—so much so that they'd pull me away from a workout class to get her. It took me a few days to notice that she cried only with a particular worker. After that realization, I made a point of calling the gym beforehand to see who was working in child care that day. If it was the person my daughter seemed to be uncomfortable with, I'd wait for her shift to end before going to the gym. My daughter at four months expressed a preference for whom she did and didn't like; I respected her preference by not forcing her to be with people who made her feel uncomfortable.

Children have boundaries unless they're shown or told it isn't okay to have them. For kids, food preference is an attempt at setting limits. They may not know what's best in terms of nutrition, but they know what they don't like. Their food preferences are based on texture, smell, color, and taste.

When a child sets a boundary such as not wanting to eat a particular type of food, how does the parent respond?

1. Offer other options (possibly along with the food the child didn't want).
2. Insist that the child eat what they said they didn't like.
3. Punish the child by not allowing them to eat anything.

Here's an idea of what the child understands about their ability to set boundaries:

Option 1: "I hear you. I want you to eat something, so I will honor your request by presenting other options."

Option 2: "Your boundaries are not important to me, and I know what's best for you."

Option 3: "You will be punished for having preferences. Do what I say."

When a child sets a boundary such as "I don't want to hug your friend," how does the parent respond?

1. Allow the child to be self-selective about whom they feel comfortable showing affection to.
2. Push the child to hug the friend.
3. Shame or threaten the child by saying "It's not nice to tell people no when they ask you for a hug," or "If you don't hug them, you'll get a spanking."

Here's an idea of what the child understands about their ability to set boundaries:

Option 1: "I hear you. If you feel uncomfortable showing someone affection, I will respect your preference."

Option 2: "Your boundaries are not important to me, and I know what's best for you."

Option 3: "You will be punished for having preferences. Don't embarrass your parents. Other people's feelings are more important than your own."

To raise healthy children, it's essential to allow them to have healthy boundaries. This can happen when we allow them to have a preference as to what they eat, what they wear, who they like, how they feel, and who they allow in their physical space.

Modeling

Children have never been very good at listening to their elders,
but they have never failed to imitate them.

—James Baldwin

Parents teach children by modeling. Parents who don't model healthy boundaries inadvertently teach kids *unhealthy* boundaries. I've worked with women who struggle to take good care of themselves. When I ask them, "Did you see your mother caring for herself?" they inevitably answer no.

These women not only don't know how to care for themselves, but they also feel severe guilt when they do practice self-care. They've been taught that self-care is selfish and would make them a bad person. They've seen their mothers personify a selfless image of womanhood, so in their attempt to be a woman, they repeat what they saw. But our mothers were burned out, too. It's just that their generation often believed that they were obligated to do everything for others without complaint.

Awareness of the need for self-care is on the rise today, and self-care is becoming acceptable. But it hasn't always been that way. Just a few decades ago, the literature on self-care was sparse. At Barnes & Noble in 2018, books about self-care outsold books on diet and exercise.

In the last few years, people have begun to learn that weight issues are often a symptom of the mental and emotional health issues they face. What many people don't realize, however, is that often, poor self-care is an issue with boundaries. When we consistently exercise, we set expectations for ourselves, defining what behaviors and habits we can and cannot accept. We won't find time to go to the gym or eat well if we don't have healthy boundaries with ourselves.

When It Isn't Okay to Say No

Children learn whether it's okay to say no from their parents. Learning is either direct or indirect. Firsthand, children see how their parents respond to being told no, either by siblings, other family members, or outside adults. The parents' response to being told no informs the child about whether it's okay to say no. If children receive the message "I cannot say no," then they will struggle with saying it.

This message doesn't have to be verbalized explicitly, such as "You cannot say no to me." A parent's reaction, such as giving the child the silent treatment, dismissing their concerns, or ridiculing the child for having a need, are all equal to communicating that saying no is not okay.

Learning from Others

Although the family is the first arena where we learn, we also learn from the other people in our lives. These include teachers, peers, television and movie personalities, and other adults.

Childhood Issues That Impact Boundaries, Such as Trauma, Abuse, or Neglect

Trauma

Trauma is any event or life experience that causes you to feel deeply distressed. These events don't have to be a firsthand experience. We can be traumatized by what we observe someone else experience. For example, if we witness domestic violence in our home, we're impacted even if we are never physically or verbally abused ourselves.

We may experience trauma as a result of

- Death of a loved one
- A bad accident

- Abuse/Neglect
- Bullying
- Abandonment
- Divorce
- An incarcerated parent

The experience of trauma shifts our brain and body into survival mode. This is one way in which unhealthy boundaries become a tool for survival. If we believe our survival hinges on our relationships, it will be exceedingly hard to set boundaries in those relationships. If we feel that we have no other options or way to get out of a particular situation, setting limits may not seem like a reasonable course of action.

Abuse

Physical abuse and emotional abuse are boundary violations. When people are unaware that this type of treatment is wrong, they may view abuse as an expected part of a relationship. Victims of physical or emotional abuse find it hard to set boundaries with their abusers.

When victims start to believe they are responsible for their abuse, or when they start to sympathize with the perpetrator, trauma bonding occurs. Trauma bonding limits our ability to set boundaries because we think we're the cause of the perpetrator's actions. People who grew up in abusive homes have a higher likelihood of developing trauma bonds later in life. Also, the longer the abusive relationship continues, the harder it is to leave.

Trauma bonding happens in families where children believe that they are responsible for what is said and done to them.

Verbal abuse example: "If I would've listened, my mom wouldn't have yelled and called me names."

Physical abuse example: "My dad had been drinking. I should've known better than to ask him for anything. He hits me when he's been drinking. I have to stay out of his way."

In adult relationships, the situation may look different, but trauma bonding can still be a part of the relationship.

Verbal abuse example: "My partner doesn't like questions; that's why he yells at me when I ask questions. I need to figure things out without pissing him off."

Physical abuse example: "When my wife is upset, she throws things at me. It's just how she deals with her rage."

When you're manipulated into believing that the abuse was your fault, it's a boundary violation. Regardless of the reason behind the abuse, it's never okay for someone to abuse you. Even if the person is a parent, partner, or someone you trust, manipulation is an essential factor. People who have been abused find it especially challenging to believe that others will be willing to meet their expectations.

Physical Neglect

This kind of neglect involves the absence of necessities or lack of care given to physical needs. Children who are physically neglected may not be adequately nourished or may appear unkempt. While we might assume the neglect is because of a lack of finances, this isn't always the case. Neglect can occur even in homes where financial resources are available.

Emotional Neglect

This is the absence of "enough" emotional attention. Emotionally neglectful loved ones can be well-meaning, so victims of neglect tend to sympathize with the neglectful person. It may seem ironic, but emotional neglect can sometimes be a result of *too much* closeness.

Enmeshment prevents us from establishing a sense of individuality. It leads us to believe that we are responsible for how others feel, so we protect and shield them from what we perceive as undesirable outcomes. But meeting the emotional needs of a parent is not a job for a child.

HERE'S A REMINDER for adults who experienced emotional neglect in childhood:

It was never your job . . .

To be the man of the house.
To be a confidant for your parent.
To take care of your siblings.
To learn things without parental guidance.
To keep the peace within a chaotic home.
To figure things out without emotional support.
To be responsible for bills when you were a kid.

Kids' boundaries are violated when kids are placed into adult roles—even when these roles happen as a result of necessity. In Justin's case, someone needed to be there to help with his younger brothers. But another adult, such as his dad or a grandparent, could have taken on that responsibility. Consider the damage done to Justin's relationship with his parents and siblings. He didn't have a normal sibling relationship with his brothers, as he was tasked with managing their needs. With his parents, he was a confidant and was unable to get his own emotional needs met by his parents.

When someone neglects us, it's hard for us to believe that they would be willing or able to accept our requests. In Chapter 8, we will dive deeper into how trauma impacts our ability to set and execute boundaries.

Thought Patterns That Stop Us from Setting Boundaries

9 Potential Reasons Why You Can't Sufficiently Set a Boundary

- You fear being mean.
- You fear being rude.
- You're a people-pleaser.
- You're anxious about future interactions after a boundary has been set.
- You feel powerless (and not sure that boundaries will help).
- You get your value from helping others.
- You project your feelings about being told no onto others.
- You have no clue where to start.
- You believe that you can't have boundaries in certain types of relationships.

You Fear Being Mean

Your biggest fear is being mean. But what is "being mean" really? When you say "I don't want to be mean," you're assuming that what you say to another person will be perceived that way. But how do you know what others see as mean? The truth is, you don't. The fear of being mean is based on the assumption that you know how the other person will view your words. But assumptions are not facts; they're hypotheses. Experiment with assuming that people will fully understand what you say.

You Fear Being Rude

How you verbalize your boundary matters. In Part 2 of this book, we'll go into depth about exactly how to state your boundaries. We tend to assume that when we declare what we expect, we can do it only by yelling or cursing. Typically, this is the case when we've reached a breaking point and have waited too long to set the boundary. But if you're proactive about it, you won't have to reach a breaking point. Then you'll be able to communicate your limits respectfully. If you've reached a boundary-breaking point, however, you can practice what to say, which will help you assertively deliver your expectations without yelling or "being rude."

You're a People-Pleaser

The hardest thing about implementing boundaries is accepting that some people won't like, understand, or agree with yours. Once you grow beyond pleasing others, setting your standards becomes easier. Not being liked by everyone is a small consequence when you consider the overall reward of healthier relationships.

People-pleasers tend to be consumed with thoughts about what others are thinking and feeling. They want to appear as good, helpful, and inviting. For people-pleasers, setting a boundary is especially hard because their worst fear is being disliked, on top of the fear of being mean or rude. These fears are often significant enough that people-pleasers would rather suffer in relationships without limits than face their fears.

You're Anxious About Future Interactions After a Boundary Has Been Set

The fear is, "Things will be awkward between us after this." Well, declaring a fear makes it so. If you state that you'll behave awkwardly during your next encounter, you *will*. What if you continued the relationship normally instead? State your boundary, and proceed with typical business. You can't control how your request is received, but you can choose to behave in a healthy way afterward. Maintaining a level of normalcy will help keep future encounters healthy. Do your part. Model the behavior you'd like to see in the relationship.

You Feel Powerless (and Not Sure That Boundaries Will Help)

You attend to every problem except the lack of healthy boundaries. You assume that even if you set one, people won't listen. You think about the worst-case scenario and become consumed with thoughts about how establishing a boundary will never help. But if you execute and uphold your boundary, it *will* work. Staying consistent is essential if you want others to adhere to your boundaries.

You Get Your Value from Helping Others

"I'm a helper." There's nothing wrong with that, but you can be a helper without being a pushover. Help people *and* set a boundary. Limits create clarity about how you are willing and able to help. After all, helpers, who are typically overwhelmed with caring for others while neglecting themselves, need boundaries, too.

You Project Your Feelings About Being Told No onto Others

You hate being told no—so much so that you hate telling other people no. It's natural to dislike it when you don't get what you want, but being told no is healthy. It's likely an indication that the other person has healthy boundaries. If you learn to manage your feelings about being told no, you will become a more sympathetic boundary-setter. But don't assume that others will feel the same way you feel. Allow people to have a response before you presume how they will feel. They might be open to your boundaries.

You Have No Clue Where to Start

Getting started is your biggest hurdle. "What do I say? What if they don't like it?" These are good questions. That's why in this book we'll address what to say, when to state your boundary, and what to do if it isn't well received. When you've practiced unhealthy boundaries for so long, it's hard to consider your options. You've grown accustomed to not having choices. While reading this book, you will gain a lot of ideas about possible boundaries that you can implement in various scenarios.

You Believe That You Can't Have Boundaries in Certain Relationships

You might think, "I can't tell my mother that I don't like ____." Instead, think, "How can I tell my mother that I don't like ____?" In every relationship, you can set boundaries. It's a matter of *how* you set them. Many people find it hardest to communicate expectations to family, but hard doesn't equal impossible. The hardest thing can be overcoming your belief that the process is complicated. Again, assuming the worst is what most often stops us from even trying.

Uncomfortable Feelings That May Arise from Setting Boundaries

Depending on your relationship to the other person, your connection to the situation, and how long you've gone without setting a boundary, you may experience discomfort (guilt, sadness, betrayal, or remorse).

Three things prolong uncomfortable feelings:

* Minimizing: This is the result of denying the impact of life events or trying to reduce their meaning. For example: "I was stood up for a date, but it doesn't matter because I had other things to do anyway."
* Ignoring: You act as though your emotions don't exist.

- Moving on too soon: When you try to push through a painful experience without feeling your emotions, you prolong the journey of recovery. Rushing the healing process will also likely lead to repeating the same mistakes.

Guilt

The number one question I'm asked about setting boundaries is "How can I set one without feeling guilty?" My immediate thought is "You can't." I know, I know—I'm a therapist; there must be something I can do to make boundaries guilt-free. But, nope, there isn't. What I *can* do is help you deal with your discomfort. I can help you feel better about saying no. Coping with discomfort is a part of the process of establishing a boundary. In Chapter 6, we will go in depth about ways to manage your discomfort around setting boundaries.

Sadness

Sometimes we feel sad because we don't want to be mean. If you see setting boundaries as mean or rude, you will be sad after setting one. It's essential to reframe the way you think about this process.

Here are a few ways to reframe:

- Boundaries are a way of advocating for yourself.
- Boundaries are a way to maintain the health and integrity of a relationship.
- Boundaries are an excellent way of saying "Hey, I like you so much. I want us to work on a few things."
- Boundaries are a way of saying "I love myself."

Reconsider the language you use to describe setting boundaries.

Betrayal

Setting boundaries is not a betrayal of your family, friends, partner, work, or anyone or anything else. *Not* setting them, however, is a betrayal of yourself. Don't betray yourself to please others. Changing the way you think about setting limits helps manage the discomfort associated with setting them.

Don't betray yourself to please others.

Remorse

"Did I say that? Oh my gosh that came out wrong." It's natural to feel like you didn't do the right thing. When we set boundaries, this happens because we think we're doing something wrong. But it isn't wrong or bad to set them. Reframe the way you think about setting boundaries, and that mental shift will help you minimize discomfort.

IN THIS CHAPTER, we talked about all the things that get in the way of your setting boundaries—the feelings, thoughts, and limitations you put on yourself and others. This process will become more natural to you when you get into the rhythm of consistently setting them.

Exercise

Grab your journal or a separate sheet of paper to complete the following exercise.

* How were boundaries taught in your family?
* Did your parents/caregivers honor your boundaries? If so, in what ways?

❋ How were your boundaries dishonored?

❋ When did you realize that setting them was an issue for you?

❋ What's your biggest challenge with setting them?

In the next chapter, we'll discuss the six types of boundaries. These six types can be applied to multiple areas of your life. Knowing the types of boundaries will help you dig deeper into how to implement them in various areas.

4

The Six Types of Boundaries

*It is necessary, and even vital, to set standards,
for your life and the people you allow in it.*
—MANDY HALE

Alex was known as "the needy one." Within ten minutes of meeting her, she would tell you her life story. She'd invite you into her life, and she expected you to do the same. When people didn't reciprocate, she thought it meant there was something wrong with them. In her attempt to connect, she quickly attached herself to others.

Eventually, a close friend told Alex that she needed space from their friendship, and another friend confirmed that Alex was an "over-sharer" and "needy." That's when Alex came to me looking for answers.

In addition to answering the written questions I always ask at the initial appointment, Alex wrote a few extra points about herself. Then she spoke fast as she tried to rush through all the details of her life. At the end of our session, I asked, "Why did you give me additional notes outside the questions I asked?"

"I wanted you to know all about me," she said.

Over the next few sessions, I learned that Alex believed the key to connection was knowing *everything* about someone. Nevertheless, she discussed events and details without much depth or reflection about her feelings. Over time, I found out why.

"My dad told me everything," she said after a few sessions. He even told Alex the details of her mother's affair. His model was "We don't keep secrets." Yet when Alex tried to share with her father, he immediately told her how to think instead of allowing her to talk.

She consistently asked him for input on her decisions because she didn't trust herself to make the "right" choices without his opinion. But he tended to be critical and dismissive of her feelings.

Alex's friends were overwhelmed by her constant need for connection and feedback about her life. Slowly, they began distancing themselves. Alex had no clue that she was violating other people's boundaries. To her, relationships meant closeness, and to be close, you had to talk often, disclose everything, and rely on others for validation. Although this was normal in her relationship with her parents, it didn't work long-term with her peers.

So our work together consisted of helping Alex identify her feelings, allow herself to make mistakes, and improve her self-esteem about her ability to make healthy decisions for herself. She had to learn how to relay the details of her life appropriately and at a reasonable pace.

In this chapter, we'll talk about the six areas of boundaries: physical, sexual, intellectual, emotional, material, and time.

Physical Boundaries

Personal space and physical touch are your physical boundaries. Your physical space is the perimeter around your body. We all have a certain level of awareness of our bodies and what feels comfortable to us, and everyone's needs in terms of physical space are different. People also have different views as to what physical touch is appropriate. These boundaries vary due to the setting, the relationship we have with the other person, and our comfort level. But we can tell people our preferences about personal space and physical touch.

Examples of Physical Boundary Violations
- Physical abuse
- Forcing hugs, kisses, or handshakes
- Standing too close
- Holding someone's hand in public when they've made it clear they're uncomfortable with public displays of affection
- Touching someone on their body in a way they deem inappropriate
- Reading someone's journal or another form of invasion of privacy

---

Setting a physical boundary sounds like this:
"I'm more of a handshaker; I don't want to hug."
"Please move back a little."
"I'm not comfortable with public displays of affection/PDAs. I'd prefer it if we saved this until we got home."
"I've asked you not to rub my back. It makes me feel uncomfortable."
"These are my private writings. Please don't look at them, because it's a violation of my privacy."

Here are a few ways to honor your physical boundaries:
1. Verbalize your need for physical distance to others.
2. Be clear with others about your discomfort with certain types of physical touch, such as hugging.

Bear in mind, however, that your boundaries are constantly changing. As your needs in life change, your expectations in your relationships will shift as well. So if you experience discomfort after an interaction with someone, it might be a sign that you need to set a physical limit. Let's say you've allowed someone you know to hug you in the past, but you suddenly find yourself feeling uncomfortable when hugged by this person. You have every right to tell them you no longer want to hug.

Sexual Boundaries

It's never okay to touch anyone's body without consent, and children can never consent to sexual acts. Touching, making sexual comments, or engaging in sexual acts without expressed consent is a violation of sexual boundaries. It's never acceptable for children to be placed in any sexual situation, even a sexual discussion in their presence. Since children can't communicate sexual limits, adults must adhere to appropriate behavior with children.

Unlike other boundaries that need to be spoken to be understood, many sexual ones are unspoken because they are the rules of society. These include rape, assault, and molestation.

Examples of Sexual Boundary Violations

- Sexual abuse, assault, or molestation
- Comments about someone's sexual appearance
- Touching in a sexually suggestive manner
- Sexual innuendos
- Sexual jokes

Setting a sexual boundary sounds like this:

"Your comments about my appearance make me feel uncomfortable."

"I'm not interested in a sexual relationship with you."

"Move your hand off my leg."

"Stop."

"Your comment isn't funny; it's sexually inappropriate."

Here are a few ways to honor your sexual boundaries:
1. Report sexual misconduct that you experienced or witnessed.
2. Don't make excuses for poor conduct.

Intellectual Boundaries

Intellectual boundaries refer to your thoughts and ideas. You're free to have an opinion about anything you want. And when you express your opinion, your words shouldn't be dismissed, belittled, or ridiculed.

However, staying mindful of what topics are appropriate versus inappropriate in a specific situation is another way of respecting intellectual boundaries. When Alex was young, her father told her that her mother had an affair. Although the information was truthful, it wasn't appropriate for Alex to know this at a young age. When a parent has an inappropriate conversation like this with a child, it's an intellectual boundary violation.

Examples of Intellectual Boundary Violations
- Calling someone names for their beliefs or opinions
- Yelling during disagreements
- Ridiculing someone for their views and thoughts
- Dismissing someone because of disagreements
- Demeaning a child's mother/father in front of a child
- Telling children about problems they aren't emotionally capable of handling

Setting an intellectual boundary sounds like this:
> "You can disagree without being mean or rude."
>
> "I don't think this is an appropriate conversation to have with a child."
>
> "I won't talk to you if you keep raising your voice."
>
> "That was a mean joke; I'm offended."
>
> "I just said something, and you dismissed me. Why?"

Here are a few ways to honor your intellectual boundaries:
1. If you're a parent, refrain from discussing adult matters with your kids.
2. Be respectful of people who are different from you.

Emotional Boundaries

When you share your feelings, it's reasonable to expect others to support you. For some of us, however, expressing emotions isn't easy. So when someone belittles your emotions or invalidates your feelings, they are violating your emotional boundaries. This can make you feel uncomfortable the next time you want to express your emotions.

Alex tried to tell her father how she felt, but he repeatedly dismissed her or told her how to feel. Eventually, she stopped sharing with him at all and began to distrust her own emotions. She wondered, "Is it right to feel sad about this?" Seeking validation, she asked her friends if what she felt was okay. Because her emotional boundaries had been violated, Alex was handicapped by the opinions of others. She didn't trust herself without feedback from other people.

With healthy emotional boundaries, you express your feelings and personal information to others gradually, not all at once. This also means you share only when it's appropriate, and you choose your confidants carefully. In an Instagram poll, I asked, "Have you ever shared a friend's secret with someone else?" Seventy-two percent said, "Yes, I've shared a secret." I received several DMs explaining why the secrets were shared. Here are a few reasons:

1. The secret was too burdensome.
2. There was a safety concern.
3. "I can't keep a secret."
4. "I tell my partner everything."

Examples of Emotional Boundary Violations
*   Sharing too much too soon (oversharing)
*   Sharing inappropriate emotional information with children
*   Emotional dumping/excessive venting
*   Pushing someone to share information they aren't comfortable sharing
*   Invalidating someone's feelings
*   Telling people how to feel, such as "You shouldn't be sad about that"
*   Minimizing the impact of something, such as "That wasn't a big deal"
*   Pushing people to move past complicated feelings swiftly
*   Gossiping about the personal details of another person's life

Setting an emotional boundary sounds like this:
   "When I share things with you, I expect you to keep them confidential."
   "I feel uncomfortable sharing my feelings. I would feel better if you acknowledged what I'm saying with a nod."
   "I hear that you have a lot of things going on. I don't feel equipped to help you. Have you considered talking to a therapist?"

"I don't feel comfortable talking about that topic."

"It isn't okay for you to tell me how I should feel. My feelings are valid."

"I will take my time processing my feelings. Don't rush me to move on."

"It's okay for me to feel how I feel in any situation."

Here are a few ways to honor your emotional boundaries:

1. Ask people if they want you to just listen, or if they're looking for feedback. This will help you determine whether or not to offer suggestions.

2. Share only with people you trust who can indeed hold space for your emotions.

Material Boundaries

Material boundaries have to do with your possessions. Your stuff is your stuff. If you decide to share your stuff, it's your choice. You also have the right to determine how others treat your possessions. If you loan a friend a tool in good condition, it's appropriate to expect the tool to be returned in the same shape. When people give you something back in worse condition, they've violated your material boundaries.

Examples of Material Boundary Violations

- Using things longer than the agreed-on time frame
- Never returning a borrowed item
- Loaning borrowed items to others without permission
- Damaging a possession and refusing to pay for it
- Returning possessions in poor condition

Setting a material boundary sounds like this:

"I will loan you money, but I expect the full amount back by
   Friday."

"I can't loan you my car this weekend."

"Be sure to return my tool in good condition."

"I can't loan you any money."

"You can borrow my suit, but if you stain it, you'll have to pay
   for dry cleaning."

Here are a few ways to honor your material boundaries:

1. Do not loan things to people who've demonstrated that they will
   not respect your possessions.
2. Share your expectations for your possessions up front.

Time Boundaries

In my experience, of the six areas listed, time is the boundary area
that people tend to struggle with the most. Time boundaries consist
of how you manage your time, how you allow others to use your
time, how you deal with favor requests, and how you structure your
free time. People with these issues struggle with work-life balance,
self-care, and prioritizing their needs. Giving up your time to others
is one significant way that you might violate your time boundaries. If
you don't have time for something that you want to do, you don't
have healthy boundaries with time.

**Examples of How We Violate Time Boundaries and How They Are
Violated by Others**

- Calling multiple times in a row for non-emergencies
- Expecting someone to drop everything in order to provide help
- Calling or sending text messages late when the recipient is
  sleeping
- Asking others to do things for free

- Overcommitting
- Having long conversations with emotionally draining people
- Requesting favors at a time when it's clear the other person isn't available
- Asking someone to stay late at work for no additional pay
- Accepting favor requests from people who won't reciprocate

Setting a time boundary sounds like this:
"I'm unable to stay late today."
"I work from nine o'clock to five o'clock, so I'm not available to chat throughout the day."
"I can't help you this weekend."
"I can help you with your taxes, but my fee is seventy-five dollars."
"I won't be able to make it to your event on Tuesday."

Here are a few ways to honor your time boundaries:
1. Before you say yes to a request, check your calendar to make sure you're not overcommitting. Don't try to squeeze in another event or task, or you'll be upset about doing so.
2. When you're busy, allow calls to go to voicemail and texts or emails to go unread until it's convenient for you to respond.

Exercise

Grab your journal or a separate sheet of paper to complete the following exercise.

When boundaries are violated, it's critical to have a conversation about what happened and how you felt about it. Because we can't control others, we must focus on what we will say or what actions we can take if the violation is repeated. Below you will find examples of each type of boundary. Read the scenario and consider what you would do or say for each.

Physical boundary example:

Your coworker enters your cubicle while you're busy completing a task. When you don't respond, your coworker persists by leaning over you at your desk.

Consider what you would do or say to set a boundary in this scenario.

Sexual boundary example:

Your friend's husband makes comments about his sexual prowess. He then begins texting you provocative innuendos, which makes you feel uncomfortable.

Consider what you would do or say to set a boundary in this scenario.

Intellectual boundary example:

You just ended a ten-year-long friendship. You're sharing your sadness about it with your partner, who says, "You have other friends. Get over it."

Consider what you would do or say to set a boundary in this scenario.

Emotional boundary example:

You tell your friend a secret, and your friend shares it with one of her friends.

Consider what you would do or say to set a boundary in this scenario.

Material boundary example:
A friend asks to borrow your shirt. The last time you loaned them a shirt, they returned it with a hole in it.

Consider what you would do or say to set a boundary in this scenario.

Time boundary example:
You're under a critical deadline at work. One of your team members asks you for help on one of their projects.

Consider what you would do or say to set a boundary in this scenario.

5

What Boundary Violations
Look Like

*People do not have to like, agree with, or understand your
boundaries to respect them.*

For the entire first year of her relationship with her boyfriend, Jamie
says they spent most days with each other and talked about their
future. They enjoyed trips together without arguing, and he was a
fantastic listener.

But if they had a bad day, he immediately withdrew his affection.
This only made Jamie crave him more. After a few days, he inevitably said all the right things to win her back.

"He's nice most of the time," Jamie told me. "But sometimes he
gets in these moods and picks at me about everything. When I don't
give him what he wants, he gives me the silent treatment and pouts."
Jamie wanted help understanding what she could do to improve their
relationship.

For five sessions, she talked about how she needed to understand
him better, develop thicker skin, and learn to communicate in a way
that worked for their relationship. I taught her some communication
skills, but she said, "Nothing works."

Jamie blamed herself for not understanding what her boyfriend wanted. She was sure she was the cause of their disputes and the lack of resolution between them.

Once I knew she was comfortable working with me, I asked, "Is it possible your boyfriend holds some responsibility in the communication issues?"

Jamie quickly defended him. "He communicates very well. He tells me exactly what he needs, but I don't do it correctly."

"Does he give you examples of what he wants you to do?"

"No, but I have an idea of what he wants based on what he says."

After she recounted a typical conversation between them, Jamie was able to acknowledge that she's often placed in a position where she "can never get anything right." For example, her boyfriend might request, "I want you to cook more at home." Then when she cooked, he'd say, "I don't like to eat this late. Why don't you cook earlier?"

Jamie would try cooking earlier, but he would then complain about what she prepared. "You don't listen to me," he would say.

Jamie was listening; however, she was just confused. Her boyfriend's mixed messages kept her second-guessing what she was supposed to do. She had lost sight of what she needed, expected, and would accept because she was continually trying to please him.

Our subsequent sessions together focused on the boundary violations that were taking place in her relationship.

Little "b" and Big "B" Violations

Boundary violations fall into two categories:

Little "b": Micro boundary violations are small violations that often occur in everyday encounters, as opposed to long-term relationships. With micro boundary violations, we aren't usually as emotionally affected. The violation doesn't spill over into the rest of our day, because we don't view the encounter as significant. Micro boundary violations can become more significant over time, how-ever, if the violations are repeated and persistent.

Examples of Micro Boundary Violations
1. You're checking out at the grocery store and notice that the cashier has an attitude. She's short with you in conversation and bags your food aggressively.
2. You're at a party, and a stranger comes up to you and starts talking. Thirty minutes go by, during which you learn so much about this person that you feel you could write a tell-all book. But not once have you gotten a word in edgewise.
3. You tell your coworker that you won't be able to make it to their birthday party. They tell you how important it is for you to be there and that everyone else is coming. Your coworker may really want you there, but they are guilt-tripping you, trying to manipulate you into showing up at the party.

Big "B": Macro boundary violations are big violations that erode the fabric of our relationships with others. These are long-standing and persistent. The frequency of the violations can even change the structure of the relationship.

Examples of Macro Boundary Violations
1. You're unable to make a decision without talking to your sister, who helps you sort through everything in your life.
2. Your friend's drinking has become your problem to manage, and you feel compelled to help every time they relapse. When you go out, you refrain from drinking because you know you'll have to care for your friend.
3. You're convinced everything that goes wrong in your relationship is your fault. Your partner has so many issues, and you need to do a better job of not triggering them.

Now that you have a few examples, let's talk about some common micro- and macroaggressions.

Little "b" Microaggressions

Microaggressions are subtle and can occur in any relationship. They include passive-aggressive behaviors meant to convey displeasure, hidden messages, or anger toward another. Whether intentionally or unintentionally, microaggressions communicate negativity.

In the early stages of her relationship, Jamie's boyfriend made small comments about how she spoke. Whenever she mispronounced a word or phrase, he mentioned it. She didn't think anything of it until it became a consistent issue in their conversations. Later, when their relationship became rocky, he used her phrasing as an example of her poor communication.

Microaggressions are commonly used in terms of race or LGBTQI+ bias, but they aren't limited to derogatory behaviors or comments based solely on race, gender, or sexual preference. Here are a few other examples:

Microaggression Examples
Racism (Judging People Negatively or in a Derogatory Manner Based on Race)
A white woman is on an elevator when a Black man gets on; she grips her purse.

Underlying issue: Belief that Black people are dangerous. Therefore, they are up to no good.

Body Shaming
Rebecca has gained ten pounds. Her mother tells her, "Send me a picture." Her mother responds, "Your face is so cute and chubby."

Underlying issue: Rebecca is gaining weight, and her mother is fat-phobic.

Racial Bias (Assumptions Based on Race)

Kevin, a Black man, is invited to an office holiday party with his mostly white coworkers. The sign-up sheet is passed around, and Kevin notices that someone volunteered him to bring fried chicken.

Underlying issue: Racial prejudice.

Gender Bias

Tina is the CEO of her company. She often receives the label of "bossy," while her male counterparts are described as influential leaders.

Underlying issue: Belief that women in powerful positions have attitude problems.

LGBTQI+ Bias

Kevin takes his partner to the office holiday party, and Kevin's co-worker says, "I didn't know you were that way. You don't act gay."

Underlying issue: Belief that gay men present as feminine.

MICROAGGRESSIONS ARE CONSIDERED harmless by the deliverer. However, microaggressions are harmful expressions of a more in-depth belief system. Though seemingly small, they have a huge impact.

Ways to Handle Microaggression

1. Assertively address what you perceive as a microaggression: "I notice that you said, 'I don't sound Black.' What does that mean?"
2. Suggest more appropriate behavior. For example, when others call her "bossy," Tina could point out that she's simply assertive and willing to lead.

Oversharing

When we overshare, it's an effort to connect to another person. But oversharing involves telling people information that's inappropriate based on the context, disclosing someone else's private information, or providing in-depth personal details in a relationship that hasn't established that level of disclosure.

The oversharer usually has no idea they've gone too far. People overshare with me in social settings a lot. Sometimes it's simply because I appear interested and allow them to talk without interruption. But I think it's usually because I'm a therapist and exude an "I like listening to problems" energy. I do enjoy listening to people share, but it can be awkward socially.

Oversharing Examples

Inappropriate Context

You've been assigned to train a new employee. Instead of learning about the job, your new coworker shares details about her problems with her ex.

Underlying issue: This personal information isn't appropriate in the context of your role as a trainer.

Someone Else's Information

Your friend's college roommate comes to visit, and the three of you hang out. While your friend is in the bathroom, her roommate tells you about the time your friend had an abortion.

Underlying issue: Your friend's roommate is sharing deeply personal information about someone else.

In-Depth Personal Information

While picking up groceries, Megan asks the cashier, "How is your day going?" The cashier starts to tell Megan about an argument she had with her boyfriend about his sex life with his ex-girlfriend.

Megan stands there listening to the story, feeling nervous and uncomfortable.

Underlying issue: The cashier's disclosure is deeply personal and not appropriate for this interaction.

OVERSHARERS ARE USUALLY clueless about how they are impacting others and violating boundaries. In an attempt to connect and build closeness, they give too much information. The oversharer often ignores the nonverbal cues from others that the conversation has gone too far.

Ways to Handle Oversharing
1. Gently redirect the person to a more appropriate topic.
2. Assertively say "Wow, this seems like a critical conversation that we should have at another time."
3. Say something like "I don't feel equipped to help with this situation. Do you mind if I change the topic of the conversation?"

Guilt Trips
Whenever Jamie tried to talk to her partner about their communication, he told her she had issues communicating her needs. He insisted that her problems in past relationships were due to her poor communication. Jamie became convinced that she was the one with the issue, so she felt terrible bringing it up to her boyfriend.

When someone intentionally tries to make you feel bad, they are guilt-tripping you. Guilt-tripping is a manipulative strategy that people use to persuade you to do what they want. They hope you'll feel bad, comply, or agree to something, even though you might not have done what they've accused you of doing.

Guilt Trip Examples

Ending Toxic Relationships

Rob had an abusive father and felt he had to end his relationship with his dad. Even within his family, he was subject to social scrutiny. Both family members and friends disagreed with his desire to terminate the unhealthy relationship. His sister said, "He's your father. You have to talk to him."

Underlying issue: Rob's sister devalued the importance of setting boundaries when a relationship is unhealthy.

Lacking Interest in Relationships with Certain People

Amy knew her boss was a "mean girl." When her boss invited her out for drinks after work, Amy declined. Her colleagues told her, "You could've at least gone out and had one drink."

Underlying issue: Amy's coworkers didn't feel confident enough to say no.

Being Particular About What You Like

You decide to bring some food for yourself to an upcoming family dinner because you know your eating preferences are different from everyone else's. Your cousin says, "Why do you need a special diet? Is the food here not good enough for you?"

Underlying issue: Your cousin is questioning your preferences and implying that you should change.

Not Pleasing Others

Carla was at a reunion lunch with friends from high school and said, "I don't want to get married or have kids." Her friend Pat said, "Everybody should have kids. Why wouldn't you want to get married? You're so nice."

Underlying issue: Pat tried to impose her values on Carla.

Saying No Without Giving an Explanation

A friend asks you, "Hey, can you help me move?" You respond no. Your friend says, "Why not? I need your help." There are times when it's okay to explain. Just be mindful of how the person has responded in the past to your explanations. If they accepted the explanation and moved on, go ahead and offer a brief reason. If explaining created a disagreement, keep your response brief.

Underlying issue: People want you to have a reason they perceive as valid.

PEOPLE WHO USE guilt trips are trying to get their needs met, but their needs may violate the requirements you have for yourself.

Ways to Handle Guilt-Tripping

1. Call it out: "Are you trying to make me feel bad about my decisions?"
2. Make the conversation about you, not them: "It's nothing personal. I just have preferences for myself."
3. Declare that you've made your decision: "Your response seems like you're trying to change my mind."

Big "B" Macroaggressions

Boundary violations that disrupt the fabric of a relationship are in the macro category. While violations occur routinely as a part of the relationship dynamic, macro violations, such as enmeshment, co-dependency, trauma bonding, and counterdependency can cause long-term damage.

Enmeshment

In enmeshed relationships, individualization is not acceptable. Neither are boundaries. These relationships thrive on each person being very similar to the other. If one person makes attempts to set limits, create new roles, or shift the dynamics, the relationship is in danger of termination.

This is enmeshment:
- Inability to be different from the other in a relationship
- Lack of individual identity
- Unclear sense of self separate from the other person
- Lack of boundaries
- Confusion between the *quantity* of time spent together versus the *quality* of the time spent together
- Oversharing
- Absorbing the emotions of the other person as your own
- Rejection by the other person if you attempt to form an individual identity

---

Enmeshed relationships violate boundaries in the following ways:

- Little personal space is given, emotionally or physically.
- The thoughts of both people must be aligned.
- Life decisions are based on mutual agreement and no independence of thought.

Sharon Martin, LCSW, defines enmeshment as "family relationships with weak boundaries, lack of emotional separation, and intrusive demands for support or attention that prevent family members from developing a strong and independent sense of self." Family relationships, dating relationships, and relationships at work can all suffer from enmeshment.

Examples of Enmeshment

You start dating someone and begin spending all your time together. Their likes become your likes. Your friends and the life you had before are suddenly diminished.

You were pretty sure you wanted to buy a new house, but after talking to your parents, you changed your mind. Your parents always know what's best for you.

Your friend is having issues with her partner. She always calls you to problem-solve their issues. You willingly help because you want her to be happy. You're even invited to speak with her partner about what you and your friend think is best for the relationship.

Boundaries for Enmeshment

- If you agree to help, ask how they plan to handle their problems in the future.
- Allow for physical space in the relationship.
- Assess your need for constant contact with another person.
- Bring other people into the mix to create additional support.
- Before you share, ask if it's the appropriate time and setting.
- Reclaim or create your self-identity, separate from anyone else's.

Codependency

In codependent relationships, we believe we must help people avoid consequences, saving them from unpleasant experiences. We think it's our role to protect them. But rather than protect, we enable the other person to continue their unhealthy behavior. We see the person we're enabling as helpless and unable to take care of themselves without us.

The term "codependent" has been around for decades and is often used when describing dysfunctional family dynamics, especially when addiction is involved. But codependency pertains to any relationship where people become emotionally entangled with the feelings and outcomes of others. In codependent relationships, it's challenging to separate what we feel from what others think and feel.

Codependency is well-meaning, but we suffer because our own needs are often unmet or unnoticed. In fact, as codependents, we have a hard time distinguishing our needs from the needs of the other person.

Enabling is a significant part of a codependent relationship. It involves supporting the unhealthy behaviors of someone through action or inaction. Codependency usually happens as a result of unhealthy boundaries.

This is codependency:
- Overextending yourself
- Avoiding discussions about real issues or problems
- Cleaning up the mess that others created for themselves
- Making excuses for the poor behavior of others
- Tending to other people's needs and neglecting your own
- Doing things for people instead of helping them do things for themselves
- Taking care of people with toxic behaviors
- Feeling as if when something happens to other people, it's happening to you
- Describing other people's problems as if they're your own
- Having difficulty existing in relationships without becoming "the rescuer"
- Troubleshooting problems for others before thinking of your own issues
- Letting people rely on you in an unhealthy way
- Having one-sided relationships

In codependent relationships, one or both parties are dependent on the other for their survival. Therefore, codependency often leads to resentment, burnout, anxiety, depression, loneliness, depletion, and severe mental health issues. Being present for someone who won't care for themselves is hard work, but codependent relationships are harmful to all parties. For the enabler, their own needs are never (or rarely) met. For the enabled, they don't learn how to meet their own needs. So both people become worse together in codependent relationships.

People who are codependent suffer from unhealthy boundaries, self-esteem issues, people-pleasing tendencies, and the need for control. By helping toxic people, they receive a sense of fulfillment.

When I was in college, I loved watching the reality-TV show *Intervention*. It's a show about families and friends trying to convince their addicted loved ones to get professional help. The people on the show usually talk about how they have enabled the addict to continue their addiction by offering money or a place to stay, for example.

In some cases, people admitted to even enabling the addict to do drugs in their homes because they felt it was safer. About halfway through the show, the friends and family members meet with a recovery coach who talks about how codependency has to stop if they want to save their loved ones. The recovery coach encourages healthy boundaries.

Examples of Codependency

When you go out with your friends, you refrain from drinking because you know they'll get drunk. You buy them drinks because you know they'll be upset with you if you don't. When your friend has had too much to drink, you drive them home and stay with them through the night to make sure they're okay. You worry about their drinking even when they don't seem to be concerned. You see the consequences of their actions, and you attempt to rescue your friends.

You've observed your sister mismanage money to such a degree that she's been unable to provide financial support to her teenage children. As a result, you've become a surrogate parent to your niece and nephew. They call you when they need something because they know their mom will say no. You help because she mismanages her money, and you don't want them to suffer because of her poor choices.

Boundaries for Codependency

- Set clear expectations with regard to how you can help.
- Provide feedback about how the other person's behaviors are affecting you.
- Support people without doing things for them.
- Wait for people to ask for help instead of offering before they ask.
- Honor your commitment to yourself about what you will and will not tolerate in relationships.
- Be vocal about toxic behaviors you observe.
- Take care of yourself.
- Hold people accountable for caring for themselves.
- Help while teaching people how to help themselves.

Trauma Bonding

Trauma bonding happens as a result of emotional and intellectual boundary violations. Over time, a person is manipulated into believing that in some way they deserve what's happening to them. They think what's done to them is by accident or not intended to harm.

Trauma bonding can occur in friendships, dating relationships, or family relationships.

This is trauma bonding:

- Being made to believe that everything is your fault (gaslighting)
- Breaking up and then going back to unhealthy relationships
- Making excuses for the other person's poor behavior toward you
- Feeling like you can't get out of a toxic relationship
- Cycling from harsh treatment to kindness
- Not telling others how you're treated in your relationship because you fear they will see it as abuse
- Not standing up to someone who mistreats you

Examples of Trauma Bonding

Jamie blamed the issues in her relationship on herself. She knew her boyfriend had problems, but she took ownership whenever he became triggered. She was afraid to share her relationship issues with her friends for fear they would judge her and her boyfriend.

Your father is verbally aggressive. He says you caused him to become angry because you didn't listen to him. After the verbal attacks, he becomes affectionate and buys you small gifts.

Your friend is mean to you in front of your other friends. You know he has a hard time in social situations, so you brush off his behavior. You believe he's mean simply because he feels uncomfortable.

Boundaries for Trauma Bonding

- Be clear about how you expect to be treated.
- Stop people immediately when they say something mean or something that makes you feel uncomfortable. Tell them "What you said makes me feel uncomfortable."
- Share your relationship issues only with people you trust.
- Act early when you notice a pattern forming.

Counterdependency

Counterdependency happens when we develop rigid boundaries to keep people at an emotional distance. Attachments to others are impaired with counterdependency, as you are trying to avoid connection, even when a relationship is healthy.

This is counterdependency:
- Difficulty being vulnerable
- Inability to ask for help
- Discomfort accepting help from others
- Disinterest in the lives of others
- Preference for doing things yourself
- Fearful of being close to others
- Emotional distance
- Quickly feeling overwhelmed when people are vulnerable
- Pushing people away when things become too serious
- Constant feelings of loneliness

Examples of Counterdependency

You meet a nice person and go on several dates with them. Everything seems to be going well, but you ghost them because they share how much they like you.

Your friend gives you a card for your birthday that is loving and tender. You don't tell your friend how the card made you feel.

Boundaries for Counterdependency
- Practice sharing details of your life with others.
- Tell people how they make you feel.
- Ask for help.
- Accept help if someone offers.

IN THIS CHAPTER, we explored micro- and macro-level boundary violations. These may be violated in any type of relationship—with coworkers, friends, family, romantic partners, and strangers. So some violations are smaller than others. When a stranger violates your physical space, one time might not be significant. But if your coworker repeatedly violates your need for physical space, it's a much bigger problem.

It's vital not to take ownership of how others treat you or to make excuses for their behavior. How they treat you is about who they are, not who you are.

Exercise

Grab your journal or a separate sheet of paper to complete the following exercise.

* How do you think your life will be different once you've established healthy boundaries?
* In what relationships have you established healthy boundaries?
* What are some specific actions you can take to improve your boundaries?

6

Identify and Communicate Your Boundaries

You don't have to be boundaryless to be loved.

For as long as Eric could remember, his father, Paul, was an alcoholic. Everyone else in their family made excuses for the drinking. Eric's mother would say, "You know he doesn't mean it," even keeping alcohol in the house for Paul despite the fact that she rarely drank herself. At family gatherings, everyone joined him in drinking, even though his behavior was always sloppy, loud, and embarrassing.

But Eric grew tired of minimizing his father's addiction, so he came to me wanting to learn how to address the issue. Eric told me about failed rehab attempts, mostly prompted by Paul's work challenges. His dad would get out of rehab and stay sober for a few weeks. But sooner or later, he would start to drink again.

Eric felt guilty because in his late teens and early twenties, he often shared a few beers with his dad. At twenty-five, however, Eric was no longer interested in drinking with him because his father always took it too far.

In our first few sessions together, Eric described what it was like to be the child of an alcoholic. He talked about how his home life was scary and unpredictable. When Paul was drunk, he became verbally aggressive. So Eric never knew what to expect when his dad came home from work. He tried to stay out of his father's way because he'd seen his older brother try to stand up to Paul, which resulted in several shouting matches.

As a child, Eric once asked his father, "Why do you drink so much?"

"Alcohol is my friend" was Paul's answer.

When I asked Eric about his current relationship with his father, he said their discussions were always all about Paul. Eric tried to make sure his dad was keeping himself busy and would ask if Paul had eaten anything. Paul frequently repeated himself, telling the same stories over and over. Occasionally, Paul would call his son in a rage and become verbally abusive. Eric never understood what prompted these rage-filled moments.

As his mother continued to make excuses for her husband, Eric's relationship with her also deteriorated. He couldn't confide in her, because she *always* took Paul's side. Trying to help his father was weighing on Eric.

The one thing Eric hadn't tried in an effort to improve his relationship with his parents was to set boundaries with them. He believed he'd set them by telling his mother, "I don't like Dad's drinking" and occasionally ignoring his father's phone calls. But I gently explained to Eric that these were passive-aggressive attempts.

When we passive-aggressively set boundaries, we say something indirectly to the other person, or we speak to someone who isn't in a position to resolve the issue. Eric was indirect with his father about his expectations. He assumed Paul would catch the hint, but his father remained clueless. Instead of being direct with his dad, Eric tried for so long to ignore his own concerns and act like everything was normal. In this way, Eric's behavior was passive-aggressive;

he acted frustrated without clearly communicating his desires to his father.

4 Ways to Unsuccessfully Communicate a Boundary
Passive

When someone is passive, they think something like this:

"I'm uncomfortable sharing my needs. Therefore, I will keep them to myself."

Being passive is denying your needs, ignoring them to allow others to be comfortable. People who communicate passively are afraid of how others will perceive their needs—maybe the other person will abandon them—so they do nothing to get their own needs met.

More examples of passiveness:

- Having an issue but not saying anything
- Allowing people to do and say things with which you disagree
- Ignoring things that are triggering for you

As we worked together, Eric expressed frustration because his mother wasn't doing anything about his father's alcoholism. He acknowledged how she passively responded to his father. She ignored the drunkenness and tried to get Eric and his brother to do the same. At family gatherings, she tried to include Paul in conversations even though his speech was slurred and he was belligerent.

Aggressive

When someone is aggressive, they might say or imply the following:

"I need you to see how you make me feel."

Aggressive communication is attacking another person with harsh, pushy, or demanding words and behaviors, instead of stating what we want. Aggressiveness demands, "I want you to see how upset you made me." When people are aggressive, they aren't considerate of how their behaviors make others feel. Intimidating people via behavior and verbal insults or assaults is offensive.

More examples of aggressiveness:

- Demeaning others to make your point
- Using yelling, name-calling, and cursing as tactics to convey your opinion
- Using the past to shame people
- Being loud and wrong (making up "facts" to pretend to be right)
- Confronting people to pick a fight
- Using cynical humor to ridicule, such as "You're fat! You know I'm just joking; stop being so sensitive."

In contrast to Eric, his brother was aggressive toward their father. He openly made reference to Paul being a drunk. As a kid, he stood up to his father by yelling back. As an adult, he started shouting matches. Bringing up old stories was another way that Eric's brother demeaned their father.

Whenever Eric tried to talk to his brother about the aggressiveness, his brother would say, "I get it from Dad." As Paul was aging, however, he wasn't as intimidating. Only occasionally would he try to shame his sons.

Passive-Aggressive

When someone is passive-aggressive, they think something like this:

"I will act out how I feel, but I'll deny how I feel." Sometimes when people act in a passive-aggressive manner, they do so unconsciously. We don't always understand the reasons behind our behavior.

In seeing clients for more than a decade, I've found that passive-aggressiveness is the number one way we communicate our feelings and needs. When people describe their passive-aggressive behavior, I say, "So you haven't communicated your need, but you've acted it out?" The problem is that people can't guess our needs based on our actions. They may not know what our behavior means or even notice that we're trying to communicate something new. Our desires simply have to be verbalized.

Passive-aggressiveness is a way we resist directly setting boundaries. To avoid confrontation, we hope the other person will figure out what they're doing wrong and self-correct their behaviors through our indirect actions. But we don't get what we want by pretending to be unbothered and avoiding the straightforward expression of our needs. Being indirect is counterproductive because our needs go unmet. This only makes us more frustrated and overwhelmed in our interactions with others.

More examples of passive-aggressiveness:

- Appearing upset but refusing to admit it
- Making verbal attacks not related to the current situation
- Being moody for no known reason (often)
- Bringing up issues from the past
- Engaging in problem-focused complaining
- Gossiping about things you could fix but have no intention of addressing

---

Eric was mostly passive-aggressive. He'd lament to his mother about his father's drinking, but other than the question he asked as a child, he'd never said anything directly to Paul about the problem. Eric ignored his father's calls sometimes, but Paul had no way of knowing this was because his son was upset. It would be easy for

Paul to assume that Eric was just too busy to answer the phone. Eric thought he'd set boundaries, but he hadn't.

Manipulation

When someone uses manipulation, they do or say things they hope will cause the other person to feel guilty and do what the manipulator wants:

"I will indirectly convince you to do what I want."

I notice "guilting" when I hear words like "convince them to _____," "make them _____," or "persuade them to _____."

It's true that manipulating people can sometimes bring results. Many adults and kids use manipulation as a way to get their needs met, pleading until they convince the other person to give in.

However, here's a way to tell the difference between manipulation and making a deal:

When making a deal, even if unfair, each party is aware of what they've agreed to do. For kids, making a deal might sound like "If I have a good day in school, will you give me a treat when I get home?" For adults, it might sound like "If I watch an action movie with you, will you watch a rom-com with me?"

The manipulated person often doesn't know they're being taken advantage of. Being manipulated feels confusing because the manipulator is trying to make the other party feel bad. Therefore, we tend to give in to things we wouldn't ordinarily agree to.

More examples of manipulation:

* Making an issue you have with them seem like an issue with you (gaslighting)
* Asking for help at the last minute and informing you that they have no other options
* Telling a story that's intended to evoke pity

- Leaving out critical parts of the story to persuade you to support them
- Withholding affection to get you to feel bad or change your behavior
- Using your relationship with them as a reason that you "should" do certain things; for example, "wives should cook," or "you should see your mother every day."

Paul manipulated his wife by talking about how stressful it was for him at work and how drinking was the only way he could unwind. When Eric spoke to his mother about Paul's drinking, she'd say, "It's so hard for him. Work is tough, and he's sensitive." She made excuses for Paul because she pitied him.

Assertiveness Is the Way

When someone is assertive, they will think something like this:

"I know what my needs are, and I will communicate them to you."

The healthiest way to communicate your boundaries is to be assertive. In contrast to all the forms of ineffective communication previously mentioned, assertiveness is how you clearly and directly state your needs.

Assertiveness involves communicating your feelings openly and without attacking others. It isn't demanding. Instead, it's a way of *commanding* that people hear you.

More examples of assertiveness:

- Saying no to anything you don't want to do
- Telling people how you feel as a result of their behavior
- Sharing your honest thoughts about your experiences

- Responding in the moment
- Instead of talking to a third party, talking directly to the person you have issues with
- Making your expectations clear up front instead of assuming people will figure them out

---

Working on boundaries means also working on your ability to be assertive. Share them without being passive, manipulative, aggressive, or passive-aggressive. If you want to set healthy boundaries, you must do so assertively.

How to Successfully Communicate a Boundary

Be assertive, and follow these three easy (well, maybe not so easy, but doable) steps.

My favorite Julia Roberts movie is *Pretty Woman*. She plays Vivian, a prostitute who falls for one of her clients, Edward (Richard Gere), a businessman. He's charming. She's skeptical. Outside, people get into both of their heads to try to stop the budding romance. But in the end, love prevails, and they live happily ever after (I hope).

Vivian isn't intimidated by the fact that Edward has more money than she does. She maintains the standards she sets for herself. One of my favorite lines is when Vivian says, "I say *who*, I say *when*, I say *how much*." She sets boundaries, and when people don't adhere to them, she honors them by leaving the situation.

Step #1

Be clear. Do your best to be as straightforward as possible. Mind your tone—don't yell or whisper. People will miss the boundary if you use complicated words or jargon. Take a deep, deep breath, and focus on being precise.

Step #2

Directly state your need or request, or say no. Don't just mention what you don't like; ask for what you need or want. Identify your expectations, or decline the offer.

Here are a few examples of steps 1 and 2 blended together:

> A friend asks you to go to a party, but you don't want to go.
> "Thanks for the invite, but I'll sit this one out."

> You're tired of hearing your friend complain about work.
> "Listen, I get that your job is frustrating. I want you to consider talking to someone in Human Resources or meeting with someone through your Employee Assistance Program to talk about your frustrations."

> Your mother gossips to you about your brother's new girlfriend.
> "I don't feel comfortable talking about her in this way. I want you to be pleasant toward her because John likes her."

> Your partner frequently mentions your weight gain.
> "I don't like it when you talk about my weight; please stop."

Eric had a difficult time identifying boundaries that he wanted to set. In talking through his family issues, he realized that he needed to set them with not just his father but also his mother and brother. Because he talked to his mom most often, he started with her. He began by setting a boundary about what bothered him the most: "When I talk about my issues with Dad, I want you to listen without defending him."

Eric felt guilty after setting the limit with his mother, and he worried that future encounters might feel awkward. At our next session, however, Eric reported that his relationship with her had improved.

He had also set a new boundary with his brother: "Please stop picking fights with Dad at family gatherings." At first, his brother denied that he was aggressive, but eventually, they had a good talk about how they'd both been impacted by their father's drinking.

Eric knew he would need more time to process what he'd say to his father. That would be the most difficult conversation for him.

Step #3

Dealing with the discomfort that happens as a result of setting boundaries is the hardest part. Discomfort is the number one reason we want to bypass setting them. It's common afterward to feel guilty, afraid, sad, remorseful, or awkward.

Guilt

The question I'm asked most often is "How do I set boundaries without feeling guilty?" There is no such thing as guilt-free boundaries. Guilt is a part of this process. Guilt typically happens as a result of thinking that what you're doing is "bad." It comes from your programming about telling people what you need or want.

From the moment many of us were born, we're made to feel guilty for having wants and needs. Some adults care for children by forcing them to ignore their boundaries. Unintentionally, caregivers may force kids to hug adults they don't want to hug. When kids don't comply with the demands of their caregivers, they're told, "You're being mean," or "That's not nice." Telling kids they're bad or mean for not complying with a request is manipulative. In these small acts, we teach children that they should feel guilty for attempting to honor their own boundaries.

For example, an adult says, "Hug me." The kid says, "I don't want to give you a hug." Then the adult says, "Well, I'm going to feel so sad if you don't give me a hug." The intention is to evoke guilt.

Some kids are trained to be seen and not heard. They're taught that asking for what they want or having healthy boundaries is disrespectful. As adults, they find it difficult to shed this outdated way of thinking. You might be called a troublemaker or the difficult one as a result.

But the bottom line is that it's okay to ask for what you want. Stating your needs is healthy. And you *can* speak up for yourself without being disrespectful.

Guilt isn't a limitation to setting boundaries. It's a feeling. And like all feelings, guilt will come and go. Try not to treat your guilt like the worst thing ever. Instead, embrace it as part of a complicated process—just one piece, not the entirety of the experience.

So how do you deal with guilt when it's present? Feel the guilt, but don't focus on it. Overfocusing on emotions just prolongs them. You can carry on while feeling guilty.

Have you ever been excited about something? Of course you have. You didn't stop everything because of it, right? You didn't miss work. You didn't stay in bed all day. You did whatever was usually on your agenda, but you felt excited at the same time. You can also carry on with your life while feeling guilty.

If you're feeling guilty, here are some reminders:
- It's healthy for you to have boundaries.
- Other people have boundaries that you respect.
- Setting boundaries is a sign of a healthy relationship.
- If boundaries ruin a relationship, your relationship was on the cusp of ending anyway.

Finally, if guilt is bothering you, engage in your favorite self-care practice, and do a few grounding techniques such as meditation or yoga.

Fear

With fear, we assume the worst. My clients say, "They're going to act weird," "I'll feel awkward," or "I may not hear from them again when I try to set my boundary." Of course we have no way of knowing how someone else will respond to our assertiveness. When someone has a history of rage and anger, it's understandable that we would avoid setting limits with that person. But we victimize ourselves further when we let our fear prevent us from doing what we need to do.

When making our expectations known, we worry about saying the right thing. The "right thing" is a matter of stating what we need through assertiveness.

In Eric's case, we went over hypothetical scenarios as to how his father might respond. Eric feared the worst—his father yelling, name-calling, and hitting walls. After all, his dad had gone into rages in the past, and for lesser offenses. Eric couldn't think of a time when anyone had imposed boundaries on his father.

Still, Eric acknowledged that his mother had imposed house rules that his dad abided by, such as taking his shoes off at the door, not smoking in the house, and going to church on Sundays. He hadn't thought of these as boundaries that his father had accepted. He could think of other rules that his father adhered to at work, in social situations, and with other members of the family. These realizations allowed Eric to see that his dad was indeed capable of honoring limits when he wanted to do so.

Sadness

"I just want to be nice." I hear this from so many people. We feel sad because we assume that setting a boundary will hurt someone's feelings. We assume that people will be unable to handle it, but this is also worst-case-scenario thinking.

Bear in mind, too, that you have no way to guess how someone else feels, so wait for them to tell you.

Sometimes you feel sad because you've wanted the people in your life to just "get it" and self-correct, understanding your needs even though you haven't stated them directly. When someone puts you in the position of having to enforce a boundary, you may not feel cared for in that relationship.

Remorse

"Did I say the wrong thing?" We wonder if we went too far, came across harshly, or even alienated the other person entirely. Immediately after stating our boundary, we may think, "What did I just say?"

It's true that words can't be unsaid. However, expressing something that's difficult can also save and improve your relationships. Be brave and state your boundary; it could change your life in numerous positive ways.

Awkwardness

"Things are going to be weird." This is a common worry as well. Remind yourself, "Just act normal." Stay grounded in the understanding that setting boundaries doesn't make you a bad person but a healthy one. Recognize that you have done something good for yourself. Do what you would typically do in the relationship. If you talk to the person daily, call them the next day. Assuming that the energy between you will become weird will create the exact uncomfortable tone you wanted to avoid. So assume that people will honor your boundaries, and act accordingly.

Ways to Communicate Boundaries

In Current Relationships
- Identify the areas in which you need limits.
- State your needs clearly.

- Don't explain yourself or provide a detailed story about what's behind your request.
- Be consistent in upholding your boundaries.
- Restate your needs when necessary.

In New Relationships

- Mention what you want casually in conversations as you're getting to know people.
- Have an open discussion about why having your needs met is important to you.
- Be clear about your expectations.
- The first time someone violates your boundaries, let them know that a violation occurred.
- Restate your needs.

Boundaries with Difficult People

Eric was sure that his father would give him a hard time. Even after he considered how his dad respected boundaries in other situations, he was unable to convince himself that his father would listen to his big ask. Eric wanted his father to stop calling when he was drunk and to stay sober at family events. Ultimately, Eric didn't want to ignore his father's drinking problem, which was tantamount to supporting it.

He decided that the first boundary would be telling his dad not to call when drunk. And he decided that waiting until the violation occurred would be the best time to bring it up. He brainstormed the exact words to use because he didn't want to stumble. He would say "Dad, I don't want to talk to you when you're drunk. I want you to call me when you're sober. I will talk to you when you're sober."

The next week, Eric couldn't wait to share with me what happened. He was half relieved and half frustrated. As soon as the boundary left his lips, his dad became defensive and denied that he was drunk. He called Eric a liar and questioned how he dared to say anything to him about what he does. Eric was completely confused about how to proceed after that explosive conversation.

Here are a few examples of people being difficult when you try to set a boundary:

Pushback
They ignore that you mentioned a boundary and continue to do what they want.

Testing Limits
They try to sneak, manipulate, or get one past you. They attempt to do what they want, but in a way you might not notice.

Rationalizing and Questioning
They challenge the reason for your boundary and its validity.

Defensiveness
They challenge what you said or your character, or make excuses about how their behavior is okay.

Silent Treatment
They stop talking to you because they didn't like what you said. This tactic is used with the hope that you'll take back your boundary.

YOU HAVE TO be okay with some of these reactions. When setting boundaries with difficult people, it's a good idea to decide beforehand how you'll deal with the potential aftermath.

For example, when someone violates your boundary, you can:

1. Assertively restate it.
2. Correct the violation in real time. Don't let the opportunity pass and then mention it later. Say it in the moment.
3. Accept that they, although difficult, are entitled to their response even if it's different from the one you'd like.
4. Decide not to take it personally. They want to do what they want to do. You're asking them to do something uncomfortable that's likely difficult for them.
5. Manage your discomfort.

Eric decided to proceed with the boundary he'd set with his father. The next time his dad called while drunk, Eric stated, "It sounds like you've been drinking. I will talk to you later." Then he promptly hung up the phone without waiting for his father's response. While staying consistent, Eric noticed that calls from his dad while drunk became infrequent. When they occurred, which wasn't often, Eric restated his boundary and hung up.

The Acclimation Period

Allow time for people to adjust to your boundaries. If you've tolerated certain problematic behaviors in the past, the other person will likely be shocked. They may say things like this:

"My drinking was never a problem before."

"Why have you changed all of a sudden?"

During the adjustment period, it's likely that you will need to repeat your boundaries, but try not to explain yourself. It's essential that you religiously uphold them. Letting violations slide because you don't feel like arguing, or it wasn't that big of a deal, will put you back at square one.

Setting boundaries is new for you and the other person. Allow both of you to acclimate to the latest standards in your relationship.

Boundary Statements: I Want . . . , I Need . . . , I Expect . . .

The best boundaries are easy to understand. Starting statements with "I need," "I want," or "I expect" helps you stay grounded in the truth of what you are.

Here are some "I want" statement examples:

I want you to stop asking me when I'm going to get married and
    have kids.

I want you to ask me what I'm feeling instead of assuming what
    I'm feeling.

Here are some "I need" statement examples:

I need you to pick up the cake for my party on time.

I need you to call me before you stop by.

Here are some "I expect" statement examples:

I expect you to show up at my graduation.

I expect you to return my car with a full tank of gas.

Follow Up On Your Boundaries with Action

We think stating boundaries is hard, but it's even harder to uphold them. People get their cues from you. If you ask them to take their shoes off in your house, you have to take your shoes off, too. If you don't, people will use your behavior as a reason for dishonoring your boundaries. So be an excellent example of the actions you request from others.

Another part of upholding the boundary you've set is deciding what you'll do if it's violated. If you do nothing, you aren't honoring your boundary.

After experiencing his initial boundary setting, Eric was ready to set the ultimate one with his father. He told Paul one week before Memorial Day, "Dad, I'm hosting a barbecue at my house. I expect you to arrive sober and not drink. If you seem to be under the influence, I will ask you to leave."

To help execute his boundary, Eric asked his mother and brother to help keep his father accountable. At the barbecue, Eric noticed that Paul was standing near the cooler with the beers. So he firmly restated his expectation to his father. Paul minimized Eric's concerns but moved away from the cooler. It wasn't easy for Eric to restate his needs, but he also felt it was beneficial for his father not to drink at the gathering.

How to Handle Habitual Boundary Violators: Which Communication Method Is Best?

State your boundary using any means necessary. I know you've probably heard that having a conversation in person is the best way to communicate it. This is certainly preferable, but texting or emailing might be the only way you feel comfortable doing it.

Still, just like in face-to-face communication, don't allow the conversation to get too detailed and convoluted. Don't go into a background story, explaining the why of it all or how long you've been feeling put upon. If you veer away from the clear and concise script, your email or text is much more likely to turn into a heated back-and-forth exchange.

So the same rules apply whether in-person or digital: always be clear by using simple and direct wording.

What to Avoid When Setting Boundaries
Never, Ever, *Ever* Apologize
In my Instagram poll, 67 percent of participants stated that they cannot set boundaries without apologizing or explaining themselves.

Don't apologize for having and setting boundaries. When you apologize, it gives the impression that your expectations are negotiable or that you don't believe you're allowed to ask for what you want. Also, if you need to say no to a request, skip the apology.

Try saying something like this:

"Thanks, but I won't be able to make it."
"I can't help you this time."
"I hope you enjoy yourself, but I won't be able to make it."

Don't Waver

Don't allow people to get away with violating your boundary even one time. That one time can quickly turn into two, three, or four times. Then you'll have to start all over.

Don't Say Too Much

Stay away from telling people the who, what, when, where, and how of your boundary. Sure, you can answer one or two questions at the most, but be intentional and succinct when you respond. Remember, people may be trying to figure out a way to change your mind. Try to stick to the original statement as much as possible.

Common Reasons People Don't Respect Boundaries

- You aren't upholding your boundaries with them.
- You didn't speak in a firm tone.
- You didn't state a need or an expectation.
- Your boundaries are flexible. One minute, they're serious; the next, they aren't.
- You assume people will self-correct even if you don't tell them what you need or want.
- You believe that stating your boundary once should be enough.
- You apologize for having boundaries.
- You issue consequences and don't stick to them.

If you want people to respect your boundaries, *you* have to respect them first.

Quick Tips for Handling Boundary Violations

Tip #1

Speak up in the moment. When you remain silent, you give people the impression that what they said or did is okay with you. What you say doesn't have to be well-thought-out or perfect. Simply say something like, "I don't like it." Saying anything is better than saying nothing.

Tip #2

Verbalize your boundaries with others. Do it organically in conversation, such as "I don't like it when people come over without calling first."

Tip #3

If someone violates a boundary you've already verbalized, tell them how the violation makes you feel. Then restate what you expect.

Tip #4

Don't let people slide—not even once.

Review of What to Say and How to Say It

There are five ways to communicate a boundary:

Passive: Letting it slide.
Passive-Aggressive: Acting upset without clearly stating your
     needs to the other person.
Aggressive: Being rigid, inflexible, and demanding about what
     you need.

Manipulation: Coercively attempting to get your needs met.

Assertive: Telling people exactly what you desire clearly and firmly.

Exercise

Grab your journal or a separate sheet of paper to complete the following exercise.

Think of a boundary you need to establish with someone.

* Write down your boundary using an "I" statement: I want, I need, I would like, or I expect. Do not write the word "because" anywhere in your sentence. Don't explain yourself, and don't apologize. It's okay to start small. Pick the boundary you'll feel most comfortable sharing.
* How do you want to share your boundary with the other person? In person, via text, or by email? Do what feels the most comfortable and appropriate.
* Go back to #1. Is your statement assertive? If so, proceed. If not, reconsider how to state your expectation.
* Decide when you want to share your boundary—now or the next time it's violated. Again, do what makes you feel most comfortable.
* Tend to your discomfort after sharing your boundary. Immediately ground yourself by engaging in a self-care practice. For example, you could meditate, write in your journal, or go for a walk.

7

Blurred Lines: Make It Plain

Boundaries are assertive steps that you take verbally and behaviorally to create a peaceful life.

Chloe was growing tired of always helping her older brother, Ray. After all, she was the "baby." Shouldn't she be the one who received the help?

She thought of Ray as a man-child who had failed to launch. He was always dependent on someone—his ex-wife, a girlfriend, their parents, or Chloe. He was manipulative—always asking to borrow money but never paying it back. Once, Chloe really needed the money back that she'd loaned him, but she had to resort to asking a friend for a loan.

She had intensely close relationships with her sister-in-law, two nieces, and one nephew from Ray's first marriage. But during his divorce, he forced Chloe to pick sides. He told Chloe that he would stop speaking to her if she continued to talk to his ex.

In my office, Chloe cried about how she wanted a "real" relationship with her brother—one based not on what she could do for him but on mutual support. She described Ray as self-centered and narcissistic. He would talk about how much he hated his ex-wife, his "awful" boss, and how much their mom got on his nerves. Chloe would listen as he complained, even though she knew most of his issues were his own fault.

She blamed their mother, who treated Ray like a prince when they were kids. Even as adults, Ray was the favorite. Whenever he didn't get his way, he had an adult tantrum, and their mother would give in. When Chloe didn't give him what he wanted, he'd tell "Mommy" on her.

She felt used and emotionally drained by her brother. Yet when he called, she almost always answered. The few times she didn't answer, she felt terribly guilty. In those moments, she could hear her mother's voice saying, "But he's your brother."

When Chloe tried to set boundaries with Ray, she'd say something like, "This is the last time I'm loaning you money." But she'd end up giving in, just like her mom did. She thought about her nieces and nephew, worrying that not helping Ray would mean that the children would be deprived.

Still, Chloe realized she needed to set boundaries with Ray, so she sought my help. She didn't understand why the ones she'd set in the past hadn't worked, and she questioned whether she should even continue her relationship with him.

Chloe knew that anything she said to their mother would be shared with Ray. So in hopes that he would hear it secondhand, she disclosed to her mom that it bothered her how Ray always made everything about himself. But Chloe never found out if Ray was told. Their mother just said, "Chloe, family is family no matter what you think of them."

"Is it okay to not *like* my family?" she asked me. She felt terrible about it, and for years had tried her best to be a "good" sister. But she was tired of being the only one trying to make their relationship healthy.

Blurred Boundaries

Blurred boundaries occur when we aren't explicitly clear about what we want, need, or expect from the other person. Instead of being direct, we may gossip or tell others what we want. We may infringe on the boundaries of others by offering unsolicited advice about how they should engage with people or by pushing our values on the other person.

Chloe was guilty of indirectly setting boundaries with Ray and gossiping about him to their mother. Also, she frequently commented on Ray's lifestyle to their mother: "He would have more money if he'd stayed with his wife," and "He wouldn't need my help if he looked for a better job." Their mom told Chloe that she "needed" to stick with family no matter what, but this was not Chloe's value for herself.

The bottom line is that blurred boundaries aren't an advantageous way to effect change in our relationships.

Blurred-Boundaries Breakdown

#1: Gossiping

In some relationships, it's customary to use gossip as a way to connect, especially with people we don't know well. Malicious gossip is when we make disparaging comments or divulge personal details about someone to whom we're close. With the intent to vent our frustrations, we share with others what we'd like to say to the person we're talking about. But the person who's listening can't help us resolve our issues with other people. In sharing personal details about another person, we passive-aggressively harm their reputation.

#2: Telling People How to Live Their Lives

Sometimes, help (solicited or unsolicited) from others comes with strings attached—"I get to tell you how to live your life." When we share a problem with someone, they may consider it helpful if they say, "You need to ____." This is a common boundary issue between adults over the age of eighteen and their parents, who struggle to stop telling their kids what they should do. It may be hard to just listen without offering advice as people share their problems, but this is often the best support we can give.

Telling people what to do with their lives doesn't allow them to work through their own issues. According to Kate Kenfield, a sex and relationship educator, "My absolute favorite question anyone asks me when I'm struggling is, 'Do you want *empathy* or a *strategy* right now?'" We often assume that others are automatically seeking our opinion about what they should do, but that isn't always the case.

In a recent Instagram poll, I asked, "When you're having an issue, what would you prefer? A: Advice or B: Listening?" More than 70 percent of the 4,000 people who answered said, "B: Listening." It seems that most of us just want to be heard.

A fundamental boundary is learning to listen without offering advice, or asking, "Do you want me to listen or offer some feedback?" Allowing people the opportunity to choose how they want you to engage is a profoundly moving way to support them as they share with you.

#3: Instructing Others as to What They Should and Shouldn't Tolerate in Relationships

"If it were me, I would ____." In relationships, we're all able to withstand different things on different levels. When we share what *we* would do if ____, it denies the other person the opportunity to decide their own boundaries. Again, just listening is a useful practice.

#4: Pushing Your Values on Others

According to Celeste Headlee, author of *We Need to Talk*: "To have important conversations, you will sometimes have to check your opinions at the door. There is no belief so strong that it cannot be set aside temporarily to learn from someone who disagrees. Don't worry; your beliefs will still be there when you're done." Everyone is entitled to their own opinion, but someone else's opinion about your life isn't more valuable than your own.

Restating/Refreshing Your Boundary

When you restate a boundary, use the same strategy as when you initially set it: be clear, state your need, and deal with your discomfort. You can't permit any violations to slide. Allowing slips will give the impression that you aren't serious about your expectations.

Chloe found it challenging to stick with her boundary. She would say, "The next time you ask me for help, I will say no." But she didn't say no. She either agreed to help or threatened to say no later. She didn't honor her boundary, because she feared the fallout: assuming that her brother would stop her from seeing her nieces and nephew, even though he'd never said he would do that.

Chloe and I decided that refreshing her boundary to something simple like "I can't help you" would be a more immediate response. I advised her to not offer an explanation or make promises about the future. She would simply say no.

Reducing Your Interactions

One of the six boundary areas is time. How often and when you give your time to others is your choice. You don't have to offer your time freely to people you find emotionally draining. It may seem like you "have to" answer the phone, respond to a text, or answer an email, but you don't. You can say no when people make requests of you, such as "Can you help me move?" It's okay to set boundaries with people who don't set any for themselves.

For Chloe, it seemed impossible to reduce her interactions with Ray. Her mother repeatedly asked her, "Have you talked to your brother?" If she said no, her mother would respond with, "Call Ray, and check on him." Their mother made it Chloe's job to maintain communication with him.

If Chloe wanted to set time boundaries with Ray, she would have to set one with her mother to stop asking that she communicate with him. Also, she wanted her mother to stop sharing her own values about the importance of family.

Luckily, setting the boundary with Ray wasn't as hard as Chloe expected. She simply stopped calling him every other day or so. Because she was initiating most of the contact, Ray didn't seem to notice at first.

The situation with her mother was more troubling. Despite being asked to stop, her mom continued to talk to Chloe about the importance of family. So Chloe needed new ways to shape the dialogue with her mother.

Issuing Ultimatums

An ultimatum is a choice given to another to either change or submit to a designated consequence. They are consequences that we intend to uphold. If an ultimatum is issued and not adhered to, it's a threat. People don't respect threats, but they can learn to respect ultimatums.

Ultimatum Examples
Statement
"I've asked you to call before you stop by. If you come over unannounced again, I won't open the door."

Action

You don't open the door when they attempt to violate your boundary.

Statement

"I don't want you to share my personal business with others. If you do, I'll stop telling you things I don't want others to know."

Action

You stop sharing with the person who violates your request for privacy.

ULTIMATUMS ARE HEALTHY when you use them as a tool to execute and follow through on your boundaries, attaching them to reasonable consequences like the ones above. Ultimatums *aren't* healthy when your consequences are punitive or when you threaten people into doing what you want.

Healthy Ultimatums

"If you aren't ready to leave by seven o'clock, I will take a taxi there without you."
"If I find out you're drinking again, I won't loan you money."
"If you don't tell me what you want for dinner, I'll decide in the next hour."

Unhealthy Ultimatums

"We need to have kids or else."
"If you go out with your friends, I'm not talking to you for the rest of the week."
"If you don't work late tonight, I'm not giving you the time off that you requested."

Chloe and I worked together to think of an ultimatum that she could stick to. She didn't want to end her relationship with her mother, because it was mostly healthy. She just wanted her mother to stop talking about Ray. So Chloe decided to say the following:

Statement

"Mom, I've asked you to stop talking about the importance of family and to stop asking me to check on Ray. As a mother, I'm sure it's difficult for you to see your children in an unhealthy relationship. But if you dishonor my boundary, I will end our conversation or change the subject. I'm not doing this to disrespect you. I'm doing this to respect myself."

Action

Chloe changed the topic or ended her conversations with her mother.

CHLOE'S CHANGE IN behavior was hard initially because she was overwhelmed with guilt. She was challenging her own beliefs about family. So she tended to her discomfort by journaling, regular therapy, finding supportive people to talk to, and using affirmations that she created to reinforce her new beliefs.

Affirming Statements

"I can have boundaries in my relationships with family."

"Setting limitations with others is a healthy way to ensure that my needs are met."

"Expressing my expectations is my way of practicing self-care."

"In healthy relationships, people will respect my wishes."

"Discomfort is a part of the process."

Some ultimatums are harder, such as those that will lead you to terminate a relationship or cut someone off. Before cutting someone off, however, consider this:

- Have I set any boundaries?
- What are some possible ways that the other person might respond to my boundaries?
- Is the other person aware of my issues with them?
- Have I been harmed beyond repair?
- Is the other person willing to repair the relationship?
- What are the healthy aspects of the relationship?

Telling People to Stop

In 90 percent of the Dr. Seuss book *Green Eggs and Ham*, Sam is asked to try green eggs and ham. In a roundabout way, he says he isn't interested, by saying things like, "I do not like them there; I do not like them anywhere." In this sixty-two-page book, Sam never says, "Stop asking me." Page after page, he's annoyed about eating something that he has clearly stated he doesn't like. When I read this book to my three-year-old, I immediately thought, "Why doesn't he just shut this down by saying 'stop'?" And guess what, around page 56, Sam agrees to eat the green eggs and ham, and he enjoys it.

People expect you to give in eventually. They continue to ask because you haven't declared in no uncertain terms that you won't give in. Saying "stop" can save you the need to repeatedly push people off. So be direct, and tell them you're not interested.

Cutoffs and Walls

Merely stating your expectations may not be enough, particularly for people who habitually violate them. Healthy boundaries include statements and actions that promote what you want in a relationship. When you set a boundary, it's your job to reinforce it.

Cutoffs

A cutoff happens when you decide to terminate an unhealthy relationship. In my Instagram Stories poll, 78 percent of people stated that they do not believe that people with unhealthy behaviors can change. If someone refuses enough times to honor your boundaries, you may choose to cut them off. Others may cut you off as well because of the limits you set with them. No matter who initiates the cutoff, it may prompt these feelings:

Relief: "I feel better without the stress of the relationship."

Regret: "I knew I shouldn't have asked them to ____."

Guilt: "It's all my fault that this happened."

Anger: "I can't believe they would respond like this."

Sadness: "I miss ____."

The above responses are normal and typical after a relationship ends, even if the response is unsatisfying.

Cutoffs happen in two ways:

1. You clearly state why you're ending the relationship with the other person.
2. You ghost the other person—leave the relationship with no warning. Ghosting is an intentional action to *passively* sever ties.

Cutoffs can be a way of caring for yourself on a deeper level, as remaining in a relationship with a person who is unwilling to change can be painful and damaging.

Walls

Walls are rigid boundaries through which you intend to protect yourself by keeping people out. With walls, the same rules apply to all people. By offering very little flexibility in your boundaries, you keep out both harmful and positive things and people. Walls are an unhealthy way of protecting yourself, as they are rigid and indiscriminate. Of course, it's essential to protect yourself from abusive or dangerous situations, but I wouldn't consider that the same as building walls. Your boundaries are made on a case-by-case basis. When you build walls, you keep everyone out, not just abusive individuals.

When someone violates your boundary, you can
- Restate or refresh it
- Reduce your interactions with that person
- Issue an ultimatum
- Accept it and let go of the relationship

Accepting and Letting Go

When you've tried setting boundaries and your requests are continuously violated, it may be time to consider cutting people off. Of course, terminating a relationship isn't easy, so put a healthy plan in place to care for yourself through the process. Ending a relationship isn't a sign that you no longer care about the other person. It's an indicator of self-love, self-care, healthy boundaries, bravery, and your desire to be well.

Terminating a relationship will mimic the grief process. You're likely to experience the following: depression, anger, confusion, and bargaining. Your ultimate goal is to come to a place of acceptance that you aren't able to change others and that you've tried to do your part in repairing the relationship.

When a relationship ends, it's okay to
- Grieve the loss (cry, be angry, feel sad)
- Practice self-compassion (it was not your fault)

- Engage in radical self-care (daily and often)
- Make a list affirming who you are (I am a loving person, etc.)
- Process what you learned about yourself as a result of the toxic relationship
- Determine how you would like to show up in your present and future relationships
- Forgive yourself for the things you allowed to happen in the relationship
- Forgive yourself for not leaving sooner

It's true—people may not like the boundaries you set, and they might retaliate by
- Cutting you off
- Giving you the silent treatment
- Manipulating you by trying to talk you out of your boundary
- Being mean

Setting limits won't disrupt a healthy relationship.

If you experience any of the above, know that the damage wasn't caused by your boundary. The relationship was already unhealthy, and your boundary brought to the surface the issues that needed to be addressed. Setting limits won't disrupt a healthy relationship.

I know it's scary to think that sharing a boundary could end a relationship. But instead of focusing on the worst-case scenario, focus on the possibility that the other person will honor your request—even if that person has been difficult in the past.

Make It Understandable the First Time

If boundary setting is a new practice for you, getting it right the first time can help you feel more confident. Stick to the script so that you're clear, direct, and to the point. That will resolve many issues with how people respond.

You may find it helpful to say that you're setting a boundary as a way of preserving the relationship. Let them know that it's healthy for the two of you. Boundaries are not the enemy.

At first, Chloe didn't honor the boundaries she set with her brother. She slipped in and out of adherence because she felt guilty or didn't want to harm her relationship with her nieces and nephew.

When we don't adhere to the limits we set with others, they won't either. Chloe struggled to stay consistent with hers, issuing an ultimatum with no intention of following through. She just hoped that her brother would get it right. But Ray knew he wouldn't receive consequences for violating his sister's boundaries.

The only thing that would resolve her issues with him would be consistency. By honoring her boundaries, Chloe could extinguish the problems she had in her relationship with Ray. She identified the following limits that she would maintain with him:

Boundary
Avoid conversations that lead you to feel emotionally drained.

Action Steps
1. Ignore calls when it isn't a good time to talk.
2. Limit the conversation to five to ten minutes.
3. Talk about yourself more.
4. Don't offer solutions; just listen.

Boundary
Cease loaning Ray money more than one time a year.

Action Steps
1. When Ray talks about finances, don't offer to help without being asked.
2. Offer a resource other than yourself.
3. Say no, and if Ray tries to evoke guilt, call him out on it: "You're trying to make me feel bad for having a boundary."
4. Make a personal financial plan, so there's no spare/extra money for Ray to borrow.

Don't just name the boundary; create realistic actions that prevent you from defaulting on it.

Sticking to your boundaries means creating new habits. In *Atomic Habits*, James Clear talks about the importance of making small changes to generate significant results: "All big things come from small beginnings. The seed of every habit is a single, tiny decision. But as that decision is repeated, a habit sprouts and grows stronger. Roots entrench themselves, and branches grow. The task of breaking a bad habit is like uprooting a powerful oak within us. And the task of building a good habit is like cultivating a delicate flower one day at a time."

So start small. You may not be ready to say no every time someone asks you to do something you don't want to do. Perhaps you could agree with yourself to say no half the time or say no to what bothers you the most. People may not recognize and adhere to your boundaries overnight. But with time, stating your expectations will become more natural to you, and people will become aware of them.

Also, instead of referring to yourself as someone who can't set boundaries, start calling yourself a "boundaried person"—even if you don't believe it at first. *You are who you say you are.* Affirming yourself as who you want to be will keep you in the mindset of making changes to implement your boundaries consistently.

Ensure That Your Boundary Was Heard

For the people in the back who pretend they didn't hear you, practice saying something like this:

"Do you understand what I requested?"

"Can you reframe what I said in your own words?"

"Just to make sure we're clear, I'd like to hear you confirm what I said."

Parents and teachers practice this all the time with the question "What did you hear me say?" Checking back is an important way to know that you were heard. It won't ensure that people will listen, but it will prevent them from saying they didn't hear or understand your stated boundaries.

When Boundaries Collide

Sasha and Toni were dating for two years when they started having heated arguments about issues related to their extended families. Toni saw Sasha's mom as rude and overbearing, and after too many power struggles, Toni vowed to maintain her distance.

Sasha was family-oriented and wanted her partner to have a close relationship with her family. While she knew her mother was over-bearing at times, she accepted her mom for who she was and didn't believe the behavior needed to be addressed.

What you want and what another person wants can sometimes be in direct opposition. For instance, Sasha wanted her partner to have a close relationship with her mother, while Toni wanted distance from Sasha's mother. In cases like this, ask yourself:

Is there any way to meet each other's boundaries halfway in a compromise?

Do either of the boundaries negatively impact the relationship? If
so, how?

Are you setting a boundary in retaliation for someone setting a
limit with you?

What are you willing to do to make sure your needs are met?

For Sasha, compromising meant accepting that her partner would
be cordial but not close to her mother. For Toni, it meant limiting the
amount of time she would spend with Sasha's mother while kindly
advocating for herself. Over time, however, this arrangement didn't
work for Sasha, and the couple decided to part ways.

In romantic relationships, your partner may not always agree
with how you handle family. When two people have colliding boundaries, it's essential to communicate clearly with one another and determine what compromises can be made. Ideally, both parties will
give a little rather than one party giving in. Perhaps Toni could have
worked toward developing a relationship with Sasha's mother and
communicating her expectations directly, and/or Sasha could have
agreed to talk with her mother about altering her behavior.

Sometimes compromises won't work, and both parties have to
agree to maintain separate boundaries and accept the other person's
stance on the matter.

IN THIS CHAPTER, we identified blurred boundaries and problems that
can arise when we aren't clear about our expectations. Ultimatums
are typically seen as negative in a relationship, but I've described some
ways to use an ultimatum to your advantage.

Also, boundaries are not walls. A wall keeps people out, while
boundaries show people how to exist in a relationship with you.

If you don't get the process of setting a boundary right the first
time, there are ways to try again.

Exercise

Grab your journal or a separate sheet of paper to complete the following exercise.

* Draw two vertical lines to make three columns.
* In column one, write a boundary you'd like to implement. It's okay to use one from the last exercise.
* In column two, write two actions to help you implement and follow up on your boundary.
* In column three, name a consequence that you can implement if your boundary isn't honored.
* Use this action plan as your mental guide when executing and following through on your boundaries.

8

Trauma and Boundaries

Free yourself from your past with healthy boundaries.

No one wanted her, so she learned to live without needing people. Amber was just one month old when she went to live with her paternal grandmother. By age ten, she'd lived with her father, grandmother, and paternal aunt—three homes with three different sets of rules.

Then, when she was ten years old, her mother came back into her life. Amber moved in with her mom and stayed there until she was seventeen.

It was hell. Amber's mother had multiple boyfriends who were jerks, and she didn't pay the bills on time, which meant they had to stay with one of the boyfriends from time to time. From ages ten to twelve, Amber was molested by her mother's then alcoholic boyfriend. When she was fifteen years old, Amber got into a physical altercation with another of her mother's boyfriends while trying to protect her mom.

At seventeen, Amber moved out on her own. She didn't want to be a burden to anyone, so she decided to take care of herself without asking anyone for anything. She didn't expect anyone to do anything for her anyway.

At thirty-two, Amber was fully independent and presented as successful. She had earned a master of business administration degree, and she had a career that she loved, mostly because it paid well.

Despite her career success, however, Amber's love life was nonexistent. Whenever she dated, her companions questioned how they could fit into her busy life. Sure, she wanted companionship, but she didn't "need" people. In relationships, she made this known by creating distance. She never allowed her partners to meet her family, and she wasn't interested in meeting their families either. She couldn't understand why people were so "clingy," wanting to talk daily and spend time with her. She abruptly cut people off before a relationship could get too serious.

So three years ago, she just stopped dating altogether. Amber believed, "I think I'm the sort of person who needs to be alone." She created her aloneness by establishing distance, ghosting people, and simply not being open to relationships.

Once in a while, Amber spoke to her parents, but not often. She usually spoke to her father only on holidays and birthdays. Her mother was married to a guy who wasn't as bad as the others, and her mom wanted to be close to her daughter. She called often and set up dates with Amber.

While she loved her mother, Amber didn't feel that she could trust her. After all, her mom wasn't there for the majority of her childhood, and she couldn't just pretend everything was okay now.

Amber had also mastered being a chameleon to accommodate whatever environment she was in. At work, she was a leader and a team player. She knew that pretending to be friendly and appearing to have it all together was necessary for her career success.

After thirty-two years of "keeping it all together," however, Amber began to experience an emotional crisis. She found herself crying at work over things that typically wouldn't bother her. She often became irritated during conversations with her mom. Usually she was able to put on a happy face, but lately she was finding herself distracted and consumed with thoughts about her childhood.

After her father died, Amber came to see me. She didn't know why she was so upset by his death. It wasn't as if they were close. But she felt outraged. It was as if her childhood trauma was resurfacing all at once. She started thinking about being abandoned by her mother, the abuse she endured, and living with various family members but never quite feeling at home in any place.

Boundaries and Trauma

Childhood trauma impacts our development, as well as our ability to implement and honor boundaries. Trauma in childhood includes sexual, physical, and emotional abuse or neglect. Let's look at each area:

The Adverse Childhood Experiences (ACE) survey was created to measure the impact of childhood trauma. The ACE measures trauma in the areas of abuse, neglect, and childhood dysfunction.

The ACE accounts for the following areas:

Abuse: physical, sexual, emotional

Neglect: physical, emotional

Household dysfunction: mental illness, incarcerated relative, substance abuse, mother treated violently, divorce (it's also traumatic to move multiple times)

People with high ACE scores, which is anything over a 4, are more prone to health issues, relationship problems, and mental health challenges such as anxiety and depression.

Amber's ACE quiz score was an 8 out of 10. On the outside, she seemed to be doing well. But internally, she was sad and lonely. She didn't have any healthy relationships, and her father had just died. All she knew was that she wanted to "feel better." She didn't want to be flooded with memories from the past or feel angry about her father's death.

When I mentioned boundaries to Amber, she had no clue what they would have to do with the issues in her life. I helped her connect how her current emotional state was attached to her childhood trauma. Slowly, she started to see how she had created rigid boundaries to keep people away.

Amber feared emotional connections. She felt weak for feeling sad and embarrassed and didn't want others to know about those feelings. Even when her dad died, she told anyone who asked that she was okay. But she wasn't okay. She was suffering in silence. And as a result of burying her emotions, all her feelings were surfacing at once.

For many months, Amber was resistant to therapy. She would come for a session, then cancel the next. She hated the idea of needing therapy to help her feel better. One day I mentioned that perhaps she *didn't* need therapy. Maybe she just needed to feel better, and therapy was a part of that process.

According to Claudia Black, a renowned addiction author, speaker, and trainer, there are three types of common boundary violations that often occur when trauma is experienced. Below are a few examples of each type.

Physical
    Inappropriate touch
    Withholding affection
    Not being taught how to care for your body
    Denying a person privacy
    Not providing proper clothing
    Hitting, pushing, pinching, shoving
    Reading private journals or going through belongings

Sexual

Sexual jokes or innuendos

Exposure to adult materials such as magazines or sexual videos

Demeaning due to one's gender (male/female) or sexual orientation

Not being given the proper information about your developing body

Forceable or coercive sexual acts

Any type of sexual abuse

Dismissing someone's request to not engage in sexual acts

Not respecting someone's desire to use protection

Emotional

Having your feelings minimized

Constantly being yelled at

Being told what to feel and how to think

Being told that your feelings are not okay

Not showing someone how to care for themselves

Being made to handle conflicts between parents

Not being given appropriate expectations

Gaslighting (blaming someone for something that wasn't their fault)

Discouraged from having an opinion

Being taunted

Directly being told that "your feelings don't matter" or "you're not enough"

Common Issues Experienced by Adults Who've Experienced Abuse or Neglect

Wanting to help everyone, even without the means to do so

Working nonstop (equating busyness with success)

Loaning people money who have proved that they won't pay
   it back

Oversharing in hopes of receiving love

Being unable to regulate emotions

Being a people-pleaser

Fearing conflict

Having low self-esteem

Being in enmeshed relationships

Being unable to make decisions without input from others

Adult Abuse

Adults can experience abuse, too, of course. In adult relationships
where domestic violence is present, there are repeated boundary violations. In relationships where adults experience verbal abuse, emotional
abuse, or emotional neglect, their boundaries are also being violated.

How Trauma Impacts Attachments

Boundary violation due to trauma, whether in childhood or adulthood, affects our ability to form healthy attachments. There are two
unhealthy attachment styles that affect boundaries in relationships:

Anxious Attachment

- Constantly seeking validation
- Engaging in self-sabotaging behavior
- Continually threatening to leave the relationship
- Frequently arguing about how committed the other person is to
  the relationship
- Breaking up often over trivial issues
- Persistently questioning actions and intent, as they are seen as a
  threat
- Having a paralyzing fear that the relationship will end
- Desiring to be close but pushing people away

- Demonstrating needy, attention-seeking behaviors
- Feeling discomfort with being alone

Avoidant Attachment
- Continually looking for reasons to justify that the relationship isn't working
- Hyperfocusing on the negative aspects of the relationship
- Being consumed with thoughts of getting out of the relationship
- Having difficulty with self-disclosure
- Constantly worrying about loss of autonomy
- Thinking "No one is good enough"
- Often feeling like a regular connection is "too clingy"

An unhealthy attachment style uses mostly rigid boundaries. People with anxious attachments, on the other hand, tend to have porous ones. Secure attachment is marked by healthy boundaries.

Secure Attachment
- Is able to be away from a partner comfortably
- Regulates emotions during disputes
- Has a healthy sense of self
- Is comfortable sharing feelings
- Allows others to express feelings without overreacting

Amber's attachment style in relationships was avoidant. Although she wanted relationships, she also wanted to be autonomous. She didn't like the feeling (or idea) of having to depend on another person. As a result of emotional neglect in childhood, a person might develop counterdependence, which is characterized as follows:

Counterdependence

- Difficulty being vulnerable with others
- Unwilling to ask for help
- Preference for doing things without help
- Discomfort with being attached to others
- Purposeful, emotional distance
- Persistent feelings of loneliness
- Inability to identify and acknowledge feelings

Counterdependence may be how someone with avoidant attachment learns to protect themselves. While there's a desire for relationships, genuinely committing to someone else feels dangerous. Therefore, they use rigid boundaries such as keeping people away or "always" saying no in order to feel safe.

Shame and Guilt After Trauma

Owning our story can be hard but not nearly as difficult as spending our lives running from it. Embracing our vulnerabilities is risky but not nearly as dangerous as giving up on love and belonging and joy—the experiences that make us the most vulnerable. Only when we are brave enough to explore the darkness will we discover the infinite power of our light.

—Brené Brown

Vulnerability is our ability to share who we are with others. We feel most comfortable being vulnerable when there is no fear of consequence. Being vulnerable allows us to be honest and open about the experiences that have shaped us. Fearing vulnerability is fearing judgment.

Growing up in a dysfunctional family may make us feel shame.

The shame leads to low self-esteem and people-pleasing. For people who have experienced trauma, the hardest part of living with it is the vulnerability of sharing the story with other people.

We fear that if we are vulnerable, people will

- Think less of us
- Hurt us again
- Minimize our trauma
- Think we're weak
- Judge us

Rigid boundaries abound when we fear vulnerability, because the mission becomes staying safe.

How Secrecy Impacts the Ability to Communicate Boundaries

When boundaries are violated, you might feel unsure about what limits are appropriate and fear whether yours will be honored.

In some families, secret-keeping is taught through sayings like "What happens in this house stays in this house." If you decide to speak about your trauma, you may feel as if you're betraying your family. In some cases, if this rule is broken, the consequence is a disruption of family relationships.

When domestic violence is present in a relationship, telling friends or family about the abuse can seem like a betrayal to your partner. You might be aware that your partner's behavior is inappropriate, but you still may not be ready to leave. Telling someone could prompt others to push you to act.

Teaching kids to keep secrets is harmful to their growth and development. The bottom line is that children and adults should be safe to talk about what happens in their homes.

How Trauma Scenarios Impact Our Ability to Implement Boundaries

#1

In your relationship with your partner, whenever you try to speak up for yourself, your voice seems offensive or "stupid." During disputes, your partner calls you names and belittles you.

Result

You may stop speaking up with your partner and others because you want to avoid conflict.

#2

As a kid, when you tried to share something with your mother, she ignored you or quickly tried to get you to stop talking. Even in cases where you may have needed support, such as issues with kids at your school, your mother wouldn't react.

Result

You developed the belief that your voice doesn't matter. Therefore, you keep things to yourself.

#3

You were sexually assaulted in college. The perpetrator said, "No one will believe you because you were drunk."

Result

You never drink again, and you don't date, because you don't trust yourself or other people.

SELF-CARE

If you've experienced codependency, sexual abuse, physical abuse, verbal abuse, emotional neglect, or physical neglect, you may have challenges with caring for yourself.

Taking care of yourself looks like

- Setting manageable expectations around caring and being present for others
- Maintaining your mental health
- Operating in your role as child instead of parent to your parents
- Operating in your role as sibling instead of parent to your siblings
- Asking for what you need
- Spending holidays doing things that you enjoy
- Giving people the space to care for themselves
- Checking in less often with people who drain your energy
- Figuring out who you are separately from what you were made to believe about yourself
- Not using your past as a reason to avoid proceeding with life
- Talking about your feelings
- Allowing yourself to feel pleasure
- Sharing the truth of your past without sugarcoating your experience
- Being gentle with yourself
- Teaching yourself things that you weren't taught in childhood
- Learning to enjoy your body

How to Work Through These Issues and Understand Them in Others

Change is possible at any time, no matter what you've experienced in life. If you notice that your boundaries are rigid, consider ways that you can create healthier ones.

For example, it's possible to change an attachment style when you're aware and ready to do the work of shifting parts of who you are. If you avoid commitment in relationships, consider the benefits of a committed relationship. Instead of continuing in a way that has felt comfortable in the past because of your trauma, decide to do something different. Start by sharing more information. Ask others for help with things that you would typically do on your own. Lean into the reciprocal nature of healthy relationships, and share yourself with another person as a way to build connections.

If you're in a relationship with someone who has attachment issues, instead of just accepting what you see, challenge it. Name what you're observing. It might even be okay to share your hypothesis of the other person's behavior. If you don't speak up, the relationship will remain unhealthy unless and until the underlying issues are addressed.

If you're in a relationship with someone who has experienced trauma, don't try to do the work for them by enabling them. Tell them what you see, and refer them to a mental health professional.

Exercise

Grab your journal or a separate sheet of paper to complete the following exercise.

❋ In what ways has your trauma impacted your ability to set boundaries?

❋ What words can you use to reassure yourself that it's okay to implement the limits and expectations that you need in order to feel safe?

9

What Are You Doing to Honor Your Boundaries?

Before we teach others to respect our boundaries,
we must learn to honor them ourselves.

Kyle received a raise, and as soon as the money hit his bank account, he was off to get a new car. As far as he was concerned, he deserved that car for all his hard work during the year. He believed in working hard and rewarding himself for it. In fact, every time he got a bonus or raise, he treated himself to a new, expensive gift—watches, designer clothes, and sometimes vacations.

Yet despite what it looked like on the outside, Kyle lived paycheck to paycheck and was drowning in twenty-five thousand dollars of credit card debt. He had no savings, and he regularly borrowed money from his father to stay afloat. He hated the idea of not being able to splurge on whatever he wanted, but he suffered the consequences of that attitude.

Kyle began seeing me at the urging of his father, following a brush with late car payments. He had agreed to get a grip on his finances. He appeared before me well dressed and intelligent, but broke.

At first, he was hesitant to open up to me because he didn't see the point. He thought that if he just got through the next few months, everything would be fine. "How often have you said that to your-self?" I asked him.

He seemed shocked. He knew he had a pattern of overspending, but he had to admit that every time his financial situation got bad, he'd say to himself, "I just need to get through the next few months." Unfortunately, those months turned into years of overspending his money and the need to be bailed out by his father. Even when Kyle made more money, he spent it on something bigger and better than what he'd had before.

Kyle was just unable to say no to himself. The thought of depriving himself made him cringe. During our second visit, I had him list his long-term financial goals. He included saving for retirement, buying a home, paying off his car, and retiring early. After he completed his list, I asked, "Now, how do you plan to meet those goals?"

Kyle spoke about how these were long-term goals, not anything he'd be able to achieve in the next year or two. After further discussion, I discovered that he'd had these same goals five years earlier, but he hadn't made any forward movement toward them.

His goals were unattainable because he had unhealthy boundaries with his finances. As long as he spent money right when he received it, he wouldn't be able to move beyond living paycheck to paycheck. Knowing that he had goals to spend his money more wisely, we began to talk about useful boundaries that might help him achieve those goals, such as saving, spending less, and delaying gratification.

The Significance of Having Boundaries with Yourself

It's hard to change your habits if you never change the underlying beliefs that led to your past behavior. You have a new goal and a new plan, but you haven't changed who you are.

—JAMES CLEAR

When we think about boundaries, we tend to think about what others need to do to make things better for us. While other people indeed have an impact on our lives, we make personal choices daily that affect the quality of our lives and who we are. With self-boundaries, we consider how *we* impact ourselves.

Kyle was choosing to be an overspender, and he was the only person responsible for it. He was the one who decided to buy things he couldn't afford, so he needed to implement boundaries for himself and his spending if he wanted to be healthier and reach his financial goals.

Kyle's financial issues are hardly unique. According to Debt.org, the average American carries a credit card balance of $8,398 and has at least four credit cards. The total U.S. consumer debt is $13.86 trillion, which includes mortgages, auto loans, credit cards, and student loans. A recent Charles Schwab study showed that 59 percent of Americans live paycheck to paycheck.

Far too many Americans live without savings, emergency funds, or retirement funds. When they experience a small financial setback, everything can fall apart.

It's a boundary issue because we lack the willingness to tell ourselves no to whatever we want. But it's dangerous to say yes to every urge without limits. This doesn't happen because we want to damage ourselves, but because we lack healthy self-boundaries.

The ability to say no to yourself is a gift. If you can resist your urges, change your habits, and say yes to only what you deem truly meaningful, you'll be practicing healthy self-boundaries. It's your responsibility to care for yourself without excuses.

Here is a list of some areas where self-boundaries are helpful:
- Your finances
- Your time management
- Your self-care

- The treatment you allow from others
- Your thoughts (yes, you can stop talking to yourself in an unkind way, just like you might stop someone else from being mean to you)
- Your reactions
- The people you allow in your life

Finances

Kyle and only Kyle can change the way he views his finances and spends his money. In our sessions, we talked about helpful beliefs versus harmful beliefs. He acknowledged that his beliefs about money were destructive, as he had to borrow money, was in debt, and struggled financially, despite making a decent income. In our work together, he began to adopt more helpful beliefs about money, such as "I don't have to spend every penny I earn."

Kyle also began creating self-boundaries, like these:

"I will save 10 percent before buying myself something new."
"I will create a budget for my spending and use the budget as a guide to curb impulse purchases."
"I will not spend more without having money saved, even if I earn more."

Kyle's new limits gave him structure around how to manage his money. Before setting these limits, he didn't think beyond the moment and suffered the consequences later. Although imposing boundaries on his finances created limitations, it also provided relief and helped Kyle move more swiftly toward his financial goals.

Another critical boundary around finances is learning when to say yes and no to others who seek to borrow or use you as a financial resource.

Boundaries to Consider
- I will not loan money to anyone if I can't afford to offer it as a gift.
- I will cosign a loan for someone only under the following conditions: ____.
- I will not cosign for anyone.
- I will establish emergency savings.

Remember, people can ask you for anything, but it's up to you to maintain your boundaries by saying no or setting limits as to how much and how little you can help them.

Time Management

A lack of self-discipline is symbolic of the lack of self-boundaries.

At this very moment, I have a screensaver on my phone that reads "I don't have time to waste time." I set this reminder to prevent myself from wasting valuable time on my phone checking social media, shopping online, and browsing the internet. It isn't wrong to do those things, but it's essential for me to use my device intentionally. I make time to use social media, shop online, and browse the internet when it makes sense for me. I just try to avoid doing it while I'm supposed to be writing a book, for example.

I love to read articles and books and listen to podcasts about time management. But truthfully, they all say the same thing: manage your distractions, plan wisely, and cut back on things that are a waste of time. Simply put, your boundaries around how you manage your time are the solution to your time-management issues.

Boundaries to Consider
- I admit to myself that I can't do everything. I will stop trying to do everything and ease into doing what I can without

overbooking myself. I will check my calendar before I say yes to any request.
- I plan to be on time by giving myself more time than I need.
- I delegate what I can, especially the things I don't need to do myself.
- I put myself on a schedule, write the schedule down, and stick to it religiously.
- I plan my day.
- I put realistic plans into place to avoid distractions.

If you struggle to manage your time, ask yourself, "What am I doing currently, versus what would I like to do instead?" Create new boundaries (habits and rules), and work toward becoming the person you'd like to be.

Self-Care

Self-care is how you nurture and restore your mind, body, and spirit. The key word here is "self," so making time to care for yourself is entirely up to you.

Don't confuse self-care, however, with treating yourself to lavish gifts and pampering yourself. In some instances you may choose for that to be a part of your regimen, but real acts of self-care have little to do with spending money. Instead, they're about showing up for yourself by setting boundaries.

Boundaries to Consider
- I say no to things I don't like.
- I say no to things that don't contribute to my growth.
- I say no to things that rob me of valuable time.
- I spend time around healthy people.
- I reduce my interactions with people who drain my energy.

- I protect my energy against people who threaten my sanity.
- I practice positive self-talk.
- I allow myself to feel and not judge my feelings.
- I forgive myself when I make a mistake.
- I actively cultivate the best version of myself.
- I turn off my phone when appropriate.
- I sleep when I'm tired.
- I mind my business.
- I make tough decisions because they're healthy for me.
- I create space for activities that bring me joy.
- I say yes to activities that interest me despite my anxiety about trying them.
- I experience things alone instead of waiting for the "right" people to join me.

Treatment We Allow from Others

"People are always taking advantage of me." I hear this frequently in my office. But are they? The real question is, How are you allowing people to take advantage of you?

It's your job to maintain the standard of how others treat you. After all, people are getting their cue from you as to what's tolerable in your relationship with them. Tell

> *How are you allowing people to take advantage of you?*

them and show them how you want to be treated, and model what you want by treating yourself well.

Boundaries to Consider

- When people raise their voice at me, I tell them it's not okay.
- I address issues when they arise instead of allowing them to fester.

- When a boundary is violated, I clearly define my expectations for communication in the beginning and throughout my relationships. Example: "I'd prefer if we talked about serious matters in person instead of over text."
- When I notice that someone is trying to manipulate me by intentionally trying to guilt me or pushing my boundaries, I recognize it as manipulation and uphold my boundaries.
- When someone says something about me that isn't true, I immediately correct them. Example: They might say, "You're always late." You might respond: "I was late today. However, there are other times, such as ____, when I've been on time." Don't argue; just state what you know to be true.

Thoughts

Yes, just like you might stop someone else from talking to you a certain way, you can stop talking to yourself in a certain way. What are your standards for how you speak to yourself—self-talk and inner dialogue—as well as how you talk about yourself in the presence of others?

It may seem corny, but giving yourself a pep talk can be beneficial.

Mantras for Self-Kindness

"It will be okay."
"I did my best."
"They didn't deserve me."

Turn that energy inward by setting a boundary to speak to yourself in a gentle, kind, and loving way.

Making self-deprecating statements is another way that you may be speaking unkindly about yourself. When you make disparaging comments or cruel jokes about yourself, you give others license to do the same to you. So be mindful of what you say about yourself in front of others.

Boundaries to Consider
- I speak to myself as gently as I would talk to a small child.
- I coach myself through awkward moments.
- I allow myself to make mistakes without judging myself harshly.
- I don't call myself names.
- I don't make mean comments about myself either in my mind or out loud in front of others.

Reactions

Make a promise to yourself to set boundaries with regard to how you respond to situations. I know this may seem difficult, since things can happen unexpectedly or people can piss you off in the moment. But just because you feel angry doesn't mean you have to yell.

Shouting is a choice you make to display that you're mad. Yet plenty of angry people make the choice to cry, take deep breaths, walk away, or phone a friend to process their feelings. You can decide how you want to deal with uncomfortable feelings and experiences.

Boundaries to Consider
- I don't hit people or any property when I'm upset.
- If I feel the need to cry, I allow myself to do so.
- When I get agitated, I remove myself from the situation and practice my breathing until I feel calm.

People You Allow in Your Life

"I always date men who cheat," Nancy said to me during a session. She had a type—a womanizer she would try to "fix." She couldn't see that in selecting the same type of man over and over, she was inviting a dynamic she claimed she didn't want.

According to the *Journal of Marriage and Family Studies*:

- 57 percent of men overall admit to committing infidelity at some point in their lives.
- 54 percent of women overall admit to committing infidelity in one or more of their relationships.
- 22 percent of married men admit to having an affair at least once during their marriages.
- 14 percent of married women admit to having an affair at least once during their marriages.

Of course, not everyone cheats. But Nancy repeatedly landed herself in relationships with men who cheated. Despite knowing the red flags of dating someone who isn't healthy, she went against her better judgment and dated guys she knew weren't good for her. Yet each time, she hoped the situation would end differently. It didn't, so she found herself asking the same question over and over: "Why does everyone cheat on me?"

The answer is that Nancy's boundaries were porous. She would allow people to do things she didn't like. Then she'd become resentful and angry. But when she came to me, she was finally ready to start a healthy relationship.

The bottom line is that you don't have to have relationships with types of people you don't like. Doing so is a choice. At least to some degree, you can curate and create the types of relationships you want by adhering to boundaries that will make your life easier. If you notice that you attract the same type of person (people) over and over, ask yourself:

What is it about me that attracts _____ type of people?

What is this person trying to teach me about myself?

What am I trying to work through in this relationship?

Boundaries to Consider

- I create an idea of the type of people I want in my life.
- When I notice issues in my relationships, I honor myself by speaking up.

Upholding Boundaries

WHEN WE WANT PEOPLE TO RESPECT OUR BOUNDARIES,

IT MAY BE NECESSARY TO REPEAT THEM.

As I've said, setting a boundary is just the first step of implementing it. The other and often more challenging step is following through if someone violates it. For example, let's say you've told your mother you'd like her to call before coming over, but she shows up without any notice. It's important to stick to your boundary by issuing a consequence. If you don't honor it by allowing your mother to violate it, she'll continue with the violation, and you'll likely feel resentful.

I know you're probably thinking, "But it's my mom! I can't issue a consequence with my mother." Yes, you can. You always have options with boundaries, even if those options make you feel uncomfortable. Perhaps you don't want to pretend you're not home. But what if you opened the door and said something like "Mom, I was clear about wanting you to call before coming. I'm not prepared for guests. Do you want to set up another time that's more convenient for both of us to hang out?"

If you don't uphold your boundaries, others won't either. You can't tell a friend "I need you to stick to our drink maximum of three drinks tonight" if you then

If you don't uphold your boundaries, others won't either.

proceed to have five drinks. In that case, you aren't modeling what you requested. Exhibit the boundaries you wish to see in the world.

Another way to uphold your boundaries is to say no more often. Recognize that saying no to others is saying yes to yourself. Set a limit by saying no when you can't honor a request, don't want to honor it, or doing so will infringe on the time you have for what you enjoy.

If you've said no, and people aren't listening, tell them to stop asking. That's right, tell them to STOP. Remember that people keep asking because they are trying to get you to eventually say yes. Also, make sure you're not leading people on by saying things like "maybe" or "I'll see," neither of which means no. If you're clear you don't want to do something, say "stop" when people continue to ask after you've said no.

Consider this:

When you engage in activities that you don't enjoy, you are taking time away from yourself.

When you get distracted with other people's stuff, you take time away from yourself.

When you spend time that you don't have to spare, you take time away from your goals.

Saying yes to yourself may look like

• Foregoing an extra hour of television when you know you need to get up early

- Staying hydrated
- Saying no to invitations you don't wish to honor
- Adhering to a monthly budget
- Taking regular breaks and not working yourself to the bone
- Going on affordable vacations
- Allowing yourself to feel your feelings without judging them as good or bad
- Setting a "do not disturb" on your phone after 8:00 p.m.
- Taking care of your physical health by going to the doctor and taking medication as prescribed
- Taking care of your mental health by going to therapy
- Resting when your body needs it
- Reading for pleasure, not with the intent to learn or grow a new skill
- Finding healthy ways to manage your emotions
- Maintaining good financial habits like paying bills on time and not racking up debt from buying things you don't need or things that can wait until you can truly afford them

---

Keeping Your Word to Yourself

Setting limits with yourself is a conscious act that will make your life easier. Rules seem restrictive, but when you create them, you can include nuance. Therefore, having boundaries with yourself is not a restriction. Instead, they help you achieve your goal, build healthy relationships, and live according to your values. When you don't keep your word to yourself, you are engaging in self-sabotage, self-betrayal, or people-pleasing.

Self-sabotage

- Procrastinating
- Getting close to a goal and quitting

- Staying in relationships that are unhealthy
- Not keeping your word to yourself
- Setting unrealistic goals
- Not trying
- Carrying a negative narrative (story) about yourself and your abilities

---

Self-sabotage is just one way that we dishonor our boundaries with ourselves. It involves engaging in unhealthy behaviors that keep us from what we say we want. Self-sabotage first starts in the way we talk to ourselves.

For example, we often talk ourselves out of trying before we even start. Once we start to talk to ourselves negatively, we commit to those negative thoughts as truth. We may say, "I can't," but we're capable of accomplishing more than we *believe* we can do. The "I can't" narrative leads to procrastination, not trying, quitting, setting unrealistic goals, and/or negative self-talk.

So in the story you tell about yourself, incorporate an "I can" narrative. Don't quit before you start. Here are some examples of what *not* to say:

- "I'm going *to try* to stop drinking for thirty days."
- "I'll see how long I can stick to drinking more water."
- "I'll share my boundary with them, but I'm one hundred percent sure they won't listen."

In other words, use direct language without ambivalence about what will happen. Here are assertive examples of self-boundary statements:

- "I'm going to quit drinking for thirty days."
- "I can change my habits."
- "I'm drinking more water, starting today."
- "I'm capable of following through."
- "Please respect my boundaries."

Confidence in your boundaries is the cure for self-sabotage.

Self-betrayal

- Changing who you are and what you believe in order to stay in relationships with others
- Pretending to be someone other than who you really are
- Comparing yourself with others (friends, family, strangers on the internet, a past version of yourself)
- Failing to consistently maintain your values
- Making negative statements about yourself to others or in your head

---

With self-betrayal, we dishonor ourselves by failing to live according to our values or failing to show up as an authentic human being. Guilt then sets in, because we know deep down that we're acting inauthentically. In healthy relationships, it's acceptable for you to be yourself.

People-Pleasing

People-pleasing is making others happy at the cost of our own happiness. It happens because we want to be accepted by others.

Those of us who are people-pleasers assume that others won't like it when we advocate for what we want. Therefore, we pretend to go along in an effort to be accepted by others. But healthy people appreciate honesty and don't abandon us if we say no.

For example, Charlotte asked me, "Is it okay for me to tell people to stop asking me when I'm getting married?" Yes! Her life isn't an open book. She doesn't have to answer any question that makes her feel uncomfortable.

It's okay to create boundaries about what you share with others. For example, you don't have to share any of the following:

- Why you aren't married yet
- Your relationship status
- When you're having a baby
- If you already have kids, when you're having more kids
- What's next in your life
- How you spend your time
- How much money you make
- How you spend your money
- Your lifestyle
- Your weight (loss or gain)
- Insert your own example here: _____
- Insert another one here: _____

You get to decide what you feel comfortable sharing as well as which people you wish to tell your personal business to. On Instagram, I'm often asked deeply personal questions, and when I don't want to answer them, I have the privilege of ignoring them.

If you don't want to answer a question, consider doing this:

- Respond with a question: "That's an interesting question; what prompted you to ask me that?"

- Turn the question back on them: "Do *you* want more kids?"
- Change the topic by glossing over the question: "Money is always such an interesting topic. What are you watching on Netflix?"
- Be direct: "I don't feel comfortable answering that question."
- Make your boundaries clear: "I don't like it when people talk to me about weight."

Remember, you have a choice about what conversations you are willing to have with others.

The Power of Refreshing and Restating Your Boundaries

Refreshing

As humans, we change, and our boundaries change with us. It's okay if your tolerance for certain things in your relationship changes. You can create new expectations. When this happens, you can say, "____ is no longer working for me; I would like ____."

You can also ease up on the boundaries you previously set. For example, if you decide you won't stay at work past 6:00 p.m., you can stay longer on occasion if you wish.

Consider this:

- What has prompted me to shift my boundaries?
- Is this a temporary or permanent shift?
- How will shifting my boundary impact my goals for myself?
- Will changing my boundary continue to honor who I am in my relationships?

Restating

Over time, people may assume that your boundaries with them have expired. Remind them (as well as yourself) about your expectations, including why they were set. Know that the changes you see in the other person are a direct result of your boundaries in the relationship.

If, over time, you find yourself reneging on the limits you set, remember how they positively impacted your life. Recommit to them, and proceed with honoring them.

You can't change people, but you can change

- How you deal with them
- What you accept
- How you react to them
- How often you interact with them
- How much space you allow them to take up
- What you participate in
- What role they play in your life
- What people you have contact with
- Who you allow in your life
- Your perspective

Consistency Is Key

From time to time, you may not honor your boundaries. But when you find yourself in a rut, get out. I know that sounds easier said than done, but remember that you don't have to commit to staying down. The moment that you begin to notice that you aren't honoring your boundaries, get right back to keeping your word to yourself.

If you've labeled yourself as a person who can't stick to things, you *will* be "a person who can't stick to things." So change the narrative of who you've told yourself you are by removing the negative connotations. Instead, say, "I'm a person who sticks to things."

The ultimate form of intrinsic motivation is when a habit becomes part of your identity. It's one thing to say I'm the type of person who wants *this. It's something very different to say I'm the type of person who* is *this.*

—JAMES CLEAR, *ATOMIC HABITS*

Exercise

Grab your journal or a separate sheet of paper to complete the following exercise.

* What type of person do you want to be? Become who you want to be, and introduce that version of yourself to the rest of the world.
* Create a list of boundaries you'd like to implement for yourself. For example, "Save more money." Next to each one, identify one actionable step to help you uphold your boundary. Example: "Start a savings account, and add $30 per month to it."

PART 2

This Is How You Do the Work of Setting Boundaries

10

Family

Tough love is you creating and keeping healthy boundaries.

James was tired of being in the middle of disputes between his mother, Debra, and his wife, Tiffany. All he wanted was for the two of them to get along. Tiffany was always complaining about his mother, and his mother was always complaining to him about how she felt hurt by Tiffany. James tried to manage both of them by listening but not picking a side.

Tiffany hated that James wouldn't put his mother in her place. He allowed his mother to act like a partner in their marriage. Every decision the couple made was run past Debra first. James did a horrible job of hiding the fact that his mother's advice persuaded his opinion. He adored her, and from his point of view, Debra was smart, successful, reliable, and offered great advice. Tiffany, on the other hand, saw Debra as manipulative, overbearing, and passive-aggressive.

Tiffany had always dreamed of having a mother-in-law who would be like a second mother to her. But from the first moment she met Debra, seven months into dating James, Debra made it clear that she was the leading lady in her son's life. James looked to his mother to help pay for their wedding and the down payment on their house, and he asked for her input on many big and small financial decisions. In their five years of marriage and two years of dating, Tiffany tried to deal with Debra by asking James to handle it, but he never put his foot down. His mother always got whatever she wanted.

Tiffany was starting to resent her husband for not standing up to his mom. As a result of that resentment, she began to withdraw, missing family events and retreating to her room when Debra dropped by. Now that James and Tiffany were thinking of starting a family, she wanted her husband to finally begin setting boundaries with his mother. Eventually, Tiffany and James decided to seek therapy to discuss how Debra was impacting their marriage.

The first few sessions were intense, as Tiffany presented issues from the past with Debra, and James defended his mother's honor. At the third session, I made the declaration, "Perhaps we should focus on just the needs of the two people present." That declaration helped us most of the time, but occasionally Debra still entered the room as a third but invisible force. When this happened, I encouraged James and Tiffany to consider the impact of a person who was not physically present but always emotionally present in the marriage. They noted that most of their disputes were due to Debra, not to anything they were doing directly to each other.

In our time together, we spoke about the importance of maintaining the integrity of the relationship by not oversharing with others. The couple created boundaries around what topics they'd like to keep between themselves, when they'd like to share certain information with others, and how they would talk about their marriage to other people.

At first, this was hard for James, because he was used to sharing everything with his mother. In the beginning, he gave in to Debra as she demanded more information in order to push her agenda. She seemed to know exactly what to say to get James to comply. After a few slip-ups, he started to prepare himself for his mother's tactics. Over time, he became firm in his expectations.

While James was learning to implement boundaries consistently,

I worked with Tiffany on using motivating language to support her husband as he shifted his relationship with his mother. He struggled with establishing himself as an adult with Debra. She had drilled into him that she knew best and wanted the best for him, and he feared that setting boundaries would push her away. He hadn't considered that he could set them with his mother while maintaining their closeness and simultaneously alleviating the issues in his marriage and the wedge between Tiffany and Debra. His mother wanted the best for James, but perhaps the best for him was having boundaries with her.

You Become an Adult When You Set Boundaries with Your Parents

Adult children are adults over the age of eighteen. Even if you live with your parents after that, you're legally an adult, and their access to your life shifts. You may, of course, have to adhere to your parents' boundaries if you're living in their household, but you can still set some of your own, even if on a smaller scale.

An essential part of becoming an adult is becoming your own guide. As you feel more comfortable being an adult, you start to lean further away from being ruled by your parents. In some cases, your parents might suggest that setting boundaries is disrespectful. But it isn't disrespectful when done with care. If you're afraid of disrespecting your parents, you might feel better sharing why the boundary is important to you.

How do you stand up to the most influential force in your life? How do you change your relationship from that of a child to that of an adult child? For your entire life, your parents have been acquainted with you inside and out. They know what to say to trigger you and get what they want. You may understand what your parents desire merely by reading their body language or noticing a shift in their mood.

Most people don't want to disappoint their parents. When I was a kid, the worst thing I ever heard from my mother was "I'm disappointed." That statement broke my heart and ensured that I would behave for at least the next two hours. Yet when you don't set boundaries with your parents, you are the one who becomes disappointed, resentful, and anxious. At some point, it's healthy for all adults to ask themselves, "What do *I* want?"

Signs That You Need Boundaries with Your Parents
- Your parents are aware of intimate details of your relationship (particularly if they're causing harm in the relationship).
- Your parents are involved with disputes you have with others.
- Your parents don't respect your opinion.
- Your parents enter your personal space without asking.
- Your parents insist that you say yes to everything.
- You say yes to your parents out of obligation even when it's inconvenient.

❋

Boundaries with your parents look like
- Expressing your feelings openly
- Managing your time in a way that works best for your schedule and lifestyle
- Not pressing yourself to attend every family event
- Giving them rules about your home
- Not allowing them to show up at your home unannounced
- Withholding intimate details of your relationship
- Not painting your partner in a negative light to your parents
- Saying no
- Introducing your partner to your parents when you're ready
- Handling your own disputes with others
- Sharing your opinion with your parents

- Being transparent with your parents about your expectations of how they can engage with your partner
- Saying no to gifts that are given with the hope of specific behavior from you
- Telling your parents that you don't want to be asked about your dating life, having kids, getting married, or any other topic that makes you feel uncomfortable
- Staying in a hotel instead of staying with family when you visit them

---

Boundaries with your parents sound like
- "I'm dating someone new. When you meet them, don't ask them when and if we're getting married."
- "I won't be home for Christmas because I've decided to celebrate with my friends."
- "Before you stop by to visit, I'd like you to call."
- "I'd like to express my feelings without being told that certain emotions aren't okay."
- "I know that you mean well and want the best for me, but I need to handle things in my relationship without your input."
- "I won't accept money from you if it comes with the intention that I do something to earn that money or that you will talk about my borrowing money."
- "I understand how important it is to you that I remain connected to my family, but I need to have my own ideas about how to maintain connections without your input."
- "When I have issues with my sister, I don't want you to get in the middle by referring to the dispute. We are adults and can resolve our differences without your guidance."
- "It makes me feel uncomfortable to hear you talk about your relationship with Mom. Please find someone else to confide in."

- "I'm vegetarian, and I'd like you to keep that in mind when you prepare meals for family gatherings."

Important Reminders
- It's normal and healthy for you to have boundaries in your relationships with people. (Remember that your parents are people.)
- Share your boundaries as soon as you notice that you need them. Doing so will prevent unwanted reactions that may occur after you've let things go on for too long.
- Setting them with your parents is new for them and for you. If there is resistance, they're likely just adjusting to this new phase in your relationship.
- Be clear and consistent when you execute your boundaries.
- It's true that you will always be your parents' child. However, you evolve into an adult with your own way of existing in the world.

Boundaries Around the Holidays

At some point in your adult life, you may decide to change your holiday traditions. Perhaps you want to celebrate at home alone, travel, or celebrate with your partner's family, etc. To establish your plans for how you want to celebrate the holiday, start early. Waiting until the last minute by putting it off may feel better to you, but letting your family know at the last minute that you're veering from the original plans might cause more issues in the family.

Boundaries around the holidays may look like
- Asking your family to stay in a hotel
- Staying in a hotel when you visit your family

- Taking some space and time to be alone if you're staying with family
- Creating new traditions
- Buying fewer gifts or sticking to a budget
- Not including people who make your holiday experience uncomfortable
- Changing the subject when heated topics are mentioned

Boundaries with Your In-Laws

If you're in a committed relationship (with or without children), it isn't uncommon for in-laws to cause stress between you and your partner. I mentioned to a client once that my mother-in-law was coming to visit, and my client asked, "Do you like her?" Of all the in-law relationships, mothers-in-law are notorious for being relationship disruptors.

In-laws disrupt the relationship when the adult child hasn't set boundaries with their parents. As a result, spouses are often left carrying the load of setting limits. The questions I'm asked most is "How do you set boundaries with someone else's parents?" In the book *Babyproofing Your Marriage: How to Laugh More and Argue Less as Your Family Grows*, authors Stacie Cockrell, Cathy O'Neill, and Julia Stone advocate for sharing your issues with your partner, mutually deciding on a course of action, and allowing your partner to execute the boundaries.

Essentially, you set boundaries with your family, and your partner sets boundaries with their family. This option works well if your partner agrees with the issues you present and feels brave in doing so with their family. If your partner hasn't established an adult child role with their parents, you may be the person left setting the limits.

If you don't set them with your in-laws, however, you may start to resent your spouse for not standing up for your relationship or for being a pushover. Speaking to your in-laws about boundaries should be done only once you've given your partner the chance to speak on your behalf.

Be kind and gentle here. Setting boundaries is tough work, and setting them with family is the hardest area for many. Your partner is struggling with something that's more than likely very difficult and scary.

Signs That You Need Boundaries with Your In-Laws

- They make your special family events (such as a wedding) about them.
- They gossip about you to their family members.
- They don't like you and have told you as much.
- They openly share their negative views of you with your children.
- They question your parenting style.
- They make decisions for your family.
- They encourage your spouse or kids to keep secrets from you.
- They hear essential things happening with your partner before you hear about it.
- They give you gifts with strings attached.
- They give your kids things they know you wouldn't want them to have.
- They don't respect the way you parent your kids.

Boundaries with your in-laws look like

- Clearly stating your parenting philosophy
- Asking your spouse to support you in a boundary you set with your in-laws
- Directly asking your partner to implement a boundary with their parent

- Not accepting gifts if you know expectations are attached
- Being transparent with your partner and children that it isn't okay to keep secrets

---

Boundaries with your in-laws sound like

To In-Law

- "We want our children to speak openly with us. Do not advise them to keep secrets from us."
- "I know that you care about our family, and I understand that you want to be involved. But it's important for us to figure out how to navigate on our own."
- "We're grateful that you're willing to help us financially. When you do so, please do it from the kindness of your heart, not with the expectation that we have to do something in return."
- "The way you parented seems different from what we're doing with our children. We ask that you respect the way we raise our kids by adhering to our wishes for them."

To Partner

- "I know you're close to your father, but don't discuss the personal details of our sex life with him."
- "When you share things with your parents first, it makes me feel left out. I would like to be the first to know what's happening with you."
- "It isn't okay for you to keep things from me and share them with your parents."
- "When I set a boundary with your parents, I'd like you to support me."

Important Reminders
- Be gentle with your partner as they learn to set boundaries with their parents.
- It's okay to share your boundary with your in-law if your partner doesn't do so.
- Don't allow boundary violations to go on too long without intervening.

Boundaries with Other Family Members

"My sister hates all my friends. Whenever I invite her anywhere with my friends, she finds a reason to have an issue with them. It's been this way since we went away to separate colleges. It's almost like she wants to be my only person." Monica was tired of trying to include her sister in plans only to have her sister ruin the moment. At her twenty-third birthday party, her sister had an argument with Monica's college roommate. Afterward, she spent most of her time at the party trying to console her sister.

Much like your parents, your other family members know how to push your buttons. Whether it's your siblings, cousins, aunts, uncles, or grandparents, they may want a prominent role in your life. It's okay for them to have a part, but you have to guide them on how you want them to show up.

Signs That You Need Boundaries with Your Other Family Members
- They use guilt trips as a way to get you to do what they want.
- They share personal stories that cause you to feel embarrassed.
- They are involved in whom you choose to date.
- They have no filter in the opinions they share about you.
- They gossip to you about other family members.
- They share your personal business with other family members.

- They push you to live a lifestyle unlike the one you want to live.
- You have codependent relationships with them.
- Your relationships are enmeshed.

Boundaries with your other family members look like
- Allowing personal distance
- Attending family events because you want to, not because you're pressured to
- Not allowing family members to comment on your dating status, weight, or any area of your life that you aren't comfortable discussing
- Identifying what you want in your relationships with family
- Creating an experience that may be different from the family norm

---

Boundaries with your other family members sound like
- "We aren't as close as we used to be, and I see that it's impacting our relationship. I will not invite you to go out with my friends if you act jealous and make the night about you."
- "We don't agree on politics. We should stop discussing politics at family gatherings."
- "I know you're concerned that I'm happy in my relationships. However, I don't want you giving me dating advice or asking me about my dating life."
- "I'm very concerned about [insert family member's name], but I will not enable them by helping pay their bills again."
- "I don't want to be in the middle of family disputes. I will no longer be the mediator."

Important Reminders

- You may be the first in your family to set boundaries; remember that doing something different may elicit an unwelcome response.
- Setting boundaries will shift how other people see you.

Boundaries with Co-Parents

"How can I survive the rest of my kids' lives with my narcissistic ex?" Jason asked me one day during a session. He shared two children with Jessica, who talked negatively about him to the kids. She also left discipline up to Jason, thereby making him appear to be the bad guy. He watched her manipulate the children by telling them how she wished she could have them more of the time, even though she'd been adamant about fifty-fifty custody.

Jason began to find it harder and harder to communicate with Jessica because she repeatedly told him that he was the one at fault for the divorce's impact on the children.

The term "co-parent" applies to coupled or uncoupled parents. Even when couples are married or separated but mostly amicable, it can be challenging to raise children with two different sets of beliefs as to how to go about it.

Parents may unknowingly affect their kids negatively by having a contentious relationship with each other. But when we have children with someone, we're forever connected to them. I know it's hard to co-parent with an ex who is difficult, but it's more comfortable when healthy boundaries are in place.

Signs That You Need Healthier Boundaries with Your Co-Parent:

- They talk about you to your children in a negative way.
- Decisions negatively impact the child because you and the other parent can't agree.

- Children witness name-calling, verbal disputes, emotional abuse, or domestic violence.
- Children are made to pick a side (choose who's right or wrong or the parent they'd like to be closest to).
- Children are used as pawns in disputes.

Boundaries with co-parents look like
- Discussing issues together before talking to the kids
- Honoring a custody agreement if one is in place
- Not sharing inappropriate information with children about the other parent
- Creating rules about how to argue in front of the children
- Using a mediator if issues can't be resolved amicably
- Assigning a pick-up and drop-off location when sending children to the other parent's home

---

Boundaries with co-parents sound like
- "While we don't see eye to eye on this, I wonder what might be a reasonable compromise."
- "I think it's best if a mediator helps us decide what's fair in terms of custody and child support."
- "Our kids shouldn't see us fighting. I won't have an inappropriate conversation in front of them."
- "Please don't speak about me and what you think of me in front of the kids."
- "The children are impacted by what they see. Let's show them how to be in healthy relationships even when we disagree with someone."

Important Reminders

- Through observing your relationship, you are teaching your kids how to exist in their own relationships.
- Children want to feel safe.
- You can only do your part. If you set a boundary, you must honor it.
- Kids greatly benefit from parents getting along.

Boundaries with Your Children

Children under the age of eighteen aren't emotionally capable of handling adult problems. Even when they're mature for their age, it isn't appropriate to share adult stressors with them. Of course, as they get older, they're capable of handling more, along with explanations to help them understand more adult concepts.

Having boundaries helps children feel safer. Despite their opposition, they benefit from rules and structure, and limits are essential to teach them how to treat others and have healthy relationships.

I will use the term "age-appropriate" several times to describe a boundary's appropriateness for different age groups. When my clients are unsure about what's age-appropriate, I ask them to look beyond what they were exposed to as children. It could be that their own experiences were inappropriate for their age.

Instead, I request that they consider TV ratings, age suggestions for specific toys, and what a doctor might say about kids safely engaging in certain things. These suggestions shouldn't be taken as hard rules, but it helps to strongly consider why they might be in place for a particular age group.

Signs That You Need Boundaries with Your Children

- They have no rules.
- Your parenting style is permissive.

- Your children are used as confidants.
- Your parenting style is punitive only.
- They are allowed to speak to others inappropriately.

Boundaries with your children look like
- Setting an age-appropriate bedtime for small kids
- Ensuring they have healthy food options available
- Discussing feelings and emotions in an age-appropriate manner
- Not using a child as a confidant
- Not expecting kids to be the caregiver for younger children in the home
- Teaching kids to take care of themselves in an age-appropriate manner
- Exposing kids to age-suitable entertainment
- Monitoring online and social media usage

Boundaries with your children sound like
- "You have school in the morning. At nine o'clock, it's time for bed."
- "Have you had any water today? No more juice until you have a few cups of water."
- "I'm the parent; I will take care of your brother."
- "Please go to your room; I need to talk to Grandma alone."
- "What you're watching is inappropriate. I'm changing settings to filter out unsuitable content."
- "It's okay to feel angry. What are some ways to behave when you feel angry?"

Important Reminders
- Even when kids seem mature for their age, it's essential to allow them to stay in a kid's reality.
- Children don't need to know the details of everything that happens with adults.
- Kids feel safe when limits are in place consistently.

Teaching Kids How to Have Healthy Boundaries

Adults often forget that children need boundaries, too. The forgetfulness is evidenced by adults blatantly either saying or acting as though "You're a kid, so no one cares about your feelings."

Adults need to remember that kids
- Have feelings and benefit significantly from being allowed to explore and express those feelings
- Are impacted by the things that adults expose them to
- Are affected by how adults respond to their problems
- Hold memories about how adults made them feel
- Aren't companions or confidants
- Lack the mental capacity to appropriately manage adult issues, no matter what their behavior reflects
- Have boundaries

Most of the adults I work with can clearly remember how their boundaries were violated in childhood and how they still struggle to repair the damage from those violations. They also struggle to incorporate healthy boundaries in their adult lives. Children must learn that having boundaries is healthy for them.

Kids are aware that they can't demand their wishes be respected, so they request that adults hear them when they make small bids for healthy boundaries.

Boundaries that a child might set sound like

- "Can you please stop saying mean things about Dad?"
- "You never pay attention to me. Why don't you just listen?"
- "I don't want to give you a hug."
- "I need you to put down your phone and spend more time with me."
- "I don't like talking to Grandma; she's always mean to me."

It's important to listen to children when they make requests like these and to honor their boundaries whenever possible.

SETTING LIMITS WITH family is particularly challenging. For years, your family has grown accustomed to you acting a certain way and playing a particular role. Change becomes necessary when you no longer want a situation to stay the way it has been. As difficult as it might seem, improving boundaries with your family is likely to create better relationships with them.

Exercise

Grab your journal or a separate sheet of paper to complete the following exercise.

❋ How do you feel about setting boundaries with your family?

❋ Who in your family do you think would be the most receptive to your boundaries?

❋ Who in your family do you think would be the least receptive to your boundaries?

❋ Name two boundaries that you'd like to implement with your family.

❋ What actions or follow-up might be necessary for your family to adhere to your boundaries?

Romantic Relationships

*We don't naturally fall into perfect relationships;
we create them.*

Malcolm and Nicole had been dating for a year before they decided to move in together. Then, after living together for two years, they found themselves constantly arguing about household duties, how much time they spent together, and the future of their relationship. Often during arguments, Malcolm would get so upset that he'd leave the house for hours. And when he returned, he'd spend the next few days giving Nicole the cold shoulder.

In our sessions, Nicole cried about their poor communication. She knew that she and Malcolm loved each other deeply, but she couldn't figure out why they argued so much.

Meanwhile, Malcolm described Nicole as "a nag." Instead of directly saying what she wanted, she was known to hint about her needs in a not-so-subtle way. This annoyed Malcolm. When irritated, he would ignore her passive-aggressive requests.

Nicole's most significant issue was that she wanted to be married. She never expected to live with Malcolm for two years without at least becoming engaged. She had become resentful, and during arguments she frequently brought up the marriage issue.

Malcolm, on the other hand, wasn't sure if he wanted to be

married. It wasn't until they'd lived together for six months that Nicole started to talk about it. Malcolm shrugged off her concerns in a way that never resolved their issues.

It was clear that these two needed help getting to the root of their problems and talking through the communication issues they commonly faced during disagreements. They thought I would referee their disputes about who was right or who should change, but to their surprise, we talked about the agreements they made with each other early in the relationship.

Beyond "I love you; you love me," Malcolm and Nicole had never talked about what each considered acceptable behavior in the relationship. Hence, Malcolm walked out during arguments. They hadn't discussed each person's expectations. Yet Nicole wanted to be married, while Malcolm was unsure. For three years, they existed with unspoken boundaries and anger about violations that were unknown to the other person.

It was clear to me from the beginning that the couple had boundary issues in their relationship.

Back to Basics

In Chapter 1, I wrote about signs that you need healthier boundaries. In this case, Nicole was resentful, and her resentment was starting to make itself known in the couple's daily interactions. Instead of communicating her needs clearly and directly, she often expressed her needs in a passive-aggressive way. She'd say, for example, "When you get back from your mom's house, I hope you have time to cook dinner like you said you would." If she was assertive, she might say something like "Be home by five o'clock so you can cook dinner for us, or grab something while you're out." Communicating her need would likely prevent an argument, but instead she set up a scenario that routinely ended in an argument.

In Chapter 2, we talked about what happens when we don't set boundaries. Nicole was burned out, so she'd say things like "I'm tired of being the one to ____" and "I'm always considering what Malcolm wants." She felt as though she was giving a lot and getting very little in return.

Malcolm wanted peace, and when his peace was disrupted by intense arguments, he set a boundary by leaving the house.

In Chapter 3, we addressed what holds people back from setting boundaries. Nicole didn't want to feel guilty for being direct about what she wanted. Also, she feared that Malcolm would be unwilling to honor her requests. Since they didn't talk issues through, however, the couple couldn't know if getting married was an option for their relationship.

In Chapter 6, we detailed ways to identify and communicate boundaries. By helping Nicole and Malcolm communicate theirs, we gave the relationship a reasonable chance of continuing on a healthy path.

As we talked through their needs, we came to the following conclusions:

Nicole's Needs

A clear understanding of the future of the relationship with the hope of one day getting married; domestic support

Malcolm's Needs

Improve how issues are identified, and address them with more meaningful communication instead of explosive disputes

FIRST, I HELPED Nicole state what she wanted clearly in a way that Malcolm could understand. To her surprise, Malcolm heard her and said he would immediately honor direct requests for more support at home. We spoke about direct ways to ask for assistance, such as

"I need your help with ____."

"Be home by five o'clock, because I'd like us to have dinner
      together."

"I scheduled a date night for us to spend some time together."

When they made clear requests, the couple noticed a reduction in the frequency and intensity of their arguments.

For the BIG conversation about marriage, Malcolm admitted to having anxiety about it because of his parents' dysfunctional relationship and other marriages he'd witnessed. They began to talk through issues and barriers, and they compromised with a new set of agreements for their relationship.

Relationship Agreements

In every relationship, we operate based on an explicit or implicit set of agreements (rules and boundaries). Based on our agreements, our relationships vary from person to person. In one relationship, we may find ourselves more argumentative; and in others, arguing isn't an acceptable practice. It isn't acceptable because at some point, an explicit or implicit agreement was made that it would be inappropriate in that relationship. For example, you might have such a spoken or unspoken agreement about arguments with your boss.

Examples of Explicit Agreements with Healthy Boundaries

"Don't raise your voice at me."

"I want an open relationship, where we discuss other partners
      with each other."

"I want to meet your friends."

Examples of Implicit Agreements with Unhealthy Boundaries

You assume that people know how to conduct themselves in a relationship with you.

You assume that people will meet your needs without your telling them what those needs are.

You assume that people automatically know your expectations.

Instead, let's assume that people know only what you tell them, honor only what you request, and can't read your mind.

Mindful Relationship Habits

- Define what it means to be in healthy relationships.
- Assess why you're in relationships with certain people.
- Notice your energy while engaging with people.
- Do what feels right for you.
- Make peace with not having a relationship that everyone agrees with.
- Challenge societal norms about what relationships should look like.
- Discover what makes you happy in your relationships.
- Honor your feelings by making healthy choices.

Setting Expectations

Set expectations at any point in your relationship, but the sooner, the better. If you want to be married, it's essential to know if the person you're dating also wants to be married. If you don't want to have kids, it's necessary to know if the person you're dating wants to have kids. From this space of clear knowing, you can create intentional agreements in your relationships that provide clarity.

It's fun at the beginning of a relationship, and we often seem easy to please. But the most pleasing thing you can do is be honest with yourself and the person you're dating. Also, to save yourself time and a lot of heartaches, believe people when they say things like "I don't want a serious relationship," "I don't think I'm the marrying type," "All my exes said I was crazy," or "I can't see myself with a kid." If you're okay with these statements, you may be equally matched. But if you want the opposite, find someone else who wants the same things. Otherwise, you'll spend most of the relationship trying to persuade the other person to want what you want. Rarely does someone change their mind to appease another person, at least not for long.

After a few dates with someone, it's an excellent time to start talking about your expectations. The biggest fear about being honest is that you might scare people away. But this is true only if they aren't interested in what you present. Therefore, as much as it might hurt, scaring them off is a sign that you're mismatched.

At the beginning of a relationship, it's vital to know
- What is the plan for the relationship?
- Do you have similar values?
- Are there any issues that are deal-breakers?
- How will you handle disputes?
- What is acceptable within the relationship?
- What unique rules do you want to implement for the relationship?

If you're deep into a relationship where boundaries weren't discussed up front, get clear about them now, and communicate them to your partner. Based on your feelings about specific issues that have come up between you, you'll know what areas you need limits in. Watch for resentment, burnout, frustration, settling, uneasiness, and anger. These emotions will guide you directly to where boundaries are needed in your relationship.

Poor Communication Is the Leading Cause of Divorce and Breakups

I've been treating couples as a relationship therapist for fourteen years. The number one reason couples seek therapy is to improve their communication. In fact, I would argue that most relationship issues boil down to communication. If you Google "books for couples," most of the books will be on this subject.

In my years of helping couples, I'm astonished by how often they operate without first discussing the rules of engagement, including what can and can't happen in the relationship. I'm not talking about what has been appropriate in other relationships, but in the current relationship. What is acceptable and unacceptable?

Here are some common areas where communication issues arise:

Fidelity
- Is your relationship monogamous?
- What does monogamy mean?
- What does cheating look like?
- What's the consequence if someone cheats?

Finances
- How will you manage your money in the relationship?
- Who is responsible for paying which bill?
- What are your short-term and long-term financial goals?
- Will you have joint or separate bank and brokerage accounts?
- Do either or both of you have financial issues?
- How will you address financial issues if they arise?

Household

- Who is responsible for doing which task?
- How will tasks be divided so that they don't fall on one person?
- How can you work together to meet the needs of your home?

Kids

- Do you want kids?
- How many kids do you want?
- What is your parenting style, or what do you think it will be?
- How will you approach disagreements related to kids?
- How will you maintain your relationship with your partner once children arrive?

Outside Forces

- How do you handle issues with your partner's family?
- What happens when you disagree with how your partner handled an issue?
- Is it okay to talk about your relationship with people outside the relationship? If so, whom?
- How do you protect your relationship from others?

Not only is it important to communicate more, but it's also important what you communicate about. Having uncomfortable conversations can save relationships. So be willing to talk about issues before they become a problem. Preventing the common communication mishaps above will save you from arguments in the future.

Having uncomfortable conversations can save relationships.

Assertiveness Minimizes Miscommunication and Recurring Arguments

Speaking up is hard, especially if your underlying belief is

- They won't care.
- They won't honor my request.
- They won't take me seriously.
- They won't understand me.
- It won't help anything.
- I don't want to be mean.

In healthy relationships, communicating your needs is welcomed and respected. In unhealthy relationships, people ignore you, push back, or even challenge your boundaries. We've already explored what to do if your relationship isn't healthy. So let's assume that your lack of assertiveness is based on fear. In my sessions with couples, I've been surprised how much they hold back from each other because they fear what the other person might say.

Janice and Sarah sought therapy because Janice wanted more sex. When I asked the couple, "How often would you like to have sex?" they both said the same thing: "Two to three times a week."

This happens so often. Why? Because instead of finding a solution, most couples quarrel about the problem. Instead of stating, "I'd like to have sex two to three times a week," then following that statement up with initiating sex, most couples resort to arguing. "We never have sex," they say.

Being assertive sets an expectation for your partner. You're no longer simply reacting to every problem; you're proactive about the issues in your relationship.

When you're faced with a challenge in your relationship, ask yourself:

1. What is the real problem?
2. What is my need?
3. How do I need to communicate with my partner?
4. What can I do to ensure that my need is met?
5. What do I want from my partner to meet my needs?

Creating an Environment for Open Communication

Open communication is a way of holding space to address issues that impact the health of your relationship or the people within it. But open communication doesn't mean that you can be mean or vent to your partner about everything you dislike. For example, you can't say things like "I hate your mother" and consider that "open." However, you might say, "I'd like to improve my relationship with your mother because I notice it's strained. Do you have any suggestions on how to do that?"

It's helpful, of course, to establish healthy communication in the beginning, but if you're already in a relationship, it's essential to talk about it now. Open communication works best when done proactively before a small issue becomes a big problem. Little things can easily add up, so address issues even when you believe them to be "not that big of a deal." You'll be surprised at the "little things" that later come up as major issues, such as

> "He takes his shoes off and leaves them right in the middle of
> the floor."
> "She never asks what I want for dinner."
> "He never takes my car to the shop. I have to do everything."

Telling your partner what you need allows them to honor your boundary. Staying quiet will piss you off.

Here are some examples and solutions for common boundary violations in romantic relationships:

"I hate my mother-in-law. My husband won't stand up to her.
What can I do?"
It may be hard to watch your husband be taken advantage of by his
mother. However, they've likely had this dynamic his entire life. You
can't make people aware of what they can't see. You might be able to
get your husband to talk more about their relationship and gently suggest small solutions for him, but the issue with your mother-in-law
won't be resolved overnight. It will take time and patience on your part.

As for your relationship with your mother-in-law, you can create
whatever boundaries you want. My only caution is to be careful not
to bad-mouth your in-laws in front of your partner when you feel
frustrated. Whatever issues you're having, you don't want to taint
your partner's relationship with their parents.

When possible, have your husband address issues with his mother
directly—and not by saying, "My wife said ____." Instead, use "we"
language, such as "We think ____." Using "we" language will make
it appear to be a joint decision instead of something that comes from
only one person.

"My partner is always late for everything."
If your boundary has been stated and not honored, you must change
your behavior to promote peace. Here are some possible options:

- Drive separately.
- Get comfortable with being late.
- Give your partner warnings.
- Accept that you're with someone who is habitually late.

"My partner loans money to family members, and I hate it."
Not loaning people money may be your rule, but not your partner's.
Here are a few options for resolving the issue:

- If your partner is using your joint accounts, you can set a rule about using only discretionary funds to help others.
- If a particular person habitually borrows, set some guidelines.
- Discuss the short- and long-term impact that loaning money has on your household.
- Talk about other ways the funds could be useful.

Difficult Periods in a Long-Term Romantic Relationship

In most marriages, people report a decline in satisfaction during the first year, soon after kids are born, and when the kids leave home.

The First Year

For many couples, learning how to coexist has its challenges, whether emotionally, from sharing the same physical space, and/or from dealing with finances. They spend the first year of marriage acclimating themselves to extended family and their many new roles and experiences.

When working with newly married couples, I notice the following three issues:

1. Learning how to navigate personal time, along with work and other life roles
2. Distributing household tasks and responsibilities
3. Managing expectations and relationships with extended family

The first year is about learning to build a life together. During this time, it's essential to be clear about your individual boundaries as well as your common ones. For example: What do you need? What do the two of you need as a couple?

Both sets of boundaries are equally important. Many couples

experience hardships in the first year simply because they haven't clearly defined their limits and expectations.

Co-Parenting

When you put two parents together, you get two different parenting philosophies. Rarely (actually, I've never seen it, but I'm hopeful) do parents agree on everything. Many couples go into parenting with the assumption that their partner will know what they need and will meet these unspoken needs.

When I was a guest on the *Whole Mamas* podcast, host Stephanie Greunke spoke about wanting to be able to prepare dinner with minimal interruptions. She expected her husband to read the situation and jump in to help. It never occurred to her to say, "While I'm preparing dinner, please take the kids upstairs and keep them engaged so that I can quickly get through the process." Instead, she suffered in silence, which, inevitably, created resentfulness.

When couples become parents, their relationship is less romantic, and they become more distant and businesslike with each other as they attend to their kids. Mundane basics like keeping kids fed, bathed, and clothed take energy, time, and resolve. In an effort to keep the family running smoothly, parents discuss carpool pickups and grocery runs instead of sharing worldviews or their thoughts on presidential elections. Questions about their day are replaced with questions about whether the diaper looks full.

These changes can be more profound than people realize. Fundamental identities may shift from wife to mother or from lovers to parents. Beyond sexual intimacy, new parents tend to stop saying and doing the little things that please their spouses. Flirty texts are replaced with messages that read like a grocery receipt.

Before having children, it's essential to communicate the importance of maintaining the integrity of romance in your relationship.

After children arrive, remember to focus on the partnership consciously. This isn't easy when kids have needs that seem more important than date night, but children benefit greatly from parents with a healthy relationship. With that in mind, make the marriage a priority.

Boundaries That Are Important for Parents
- Having consistent date nights
- Scouting repeatable babysitters for personal and couple time
- Asking for help from family
- Assigning kids a bedtime
- Prioritizing time to talk about topics other than the kids

The Empty Nest

When children leave home, parents who have built their identity around parenting may find it challenging to adjust to an empty nest. It can be particularly difficult to shift the focus back to the romantic partnership. But having kids isn't a reason to abandon yourself and your marriage. When you become a parent, you *add* kids to your life. You don't give up your life to parent children.

If porous or rigid boundaries prohibited you from having a healthy partnership, set healthy boundaries now. Commit to getting to know your spouse again, date each other, and spend time together. You can't re-create what you had before, but you can create something new.

The Curse of Poor Communication

As I said, the biggest issue with most romantic relationships is poor communication. If people could learn to communicate what they want earlier in the dating process, many relationships would be happier. A failure to communicate is a missed opportunity to have your needs met. The number one reason that people fail to communicate their needs is the fear of being seen as mean or needy.

But it's okay to have needs, and it's reasonable to think that your partner would be willing to meet most of your needs. So state them early, because resentment leads to breakups and divorce.

Needs Within Reason

That said, it isn't the responsibility of one person to fulfill every need you have. For instance, if your partner tends to offer you advice when you just want someone to listen, it may be more helpful to share with a friend. We can't change people or convince them to be different from the core of who they are, and some needs may feel to your partner like an attempt to change them. In your relationships, it's essential to consider if your request is reasonable. Requests are unreasonable when the other person can't meet the need. For example, an unreasonable request could sound like "You can never bring up the past." A reasonable request might sound like "If you bring up the past, I will verbalize that you're crossing a boundary, and I will redirect the conversation."

Exercise

Grab your journal or a separate sheet of paper to complete the following exercise.

If you're single, ask yourself:

❉ What are my top five needs in a relationship?
❉ When will I communicate my boundaries?

❋ How will I naturally communicate them?

❋ What issues will be hardest for me to set boundaries for?

❋ How would I like a potential partner to receive my boundaries?

If you're in a relationship, ask yourself:

❋ What are my top five needs in my relationship?

❋ Is my partner aware of my needs?

❋ What is the biggest issue in my relationship?

❋ Have I set any boundaries with my partner?

❋ Am I honoring the boundaries I set with my partner?

❋ In what new ways can I share my boundaries with my partner?

12

Friendships

Your boundaries are a reflection of how willing you are to advocate for the life that you want.

"I hate my job," Dave told his friend Kevin on their way home from work. As Kevin listened to Dave complain about his workday, his wife, and people in general, he felt drained and stuck. He loved his friend, but every time Dave called, Kevin took a deep breath before answering. He knew what was in store. At least twice a week, he participated in a one-sided conversation with Dave.

Yet whenever Kevin needed something, it was Dave who showed up to help. They'd been best friends since high school, and despite not going to the same college, they kept in touch. Since both of them had a thirty-minute drive home, they got into the rhythm of talking twice a week and texting throughout the day.

Kevin thought Dave was funny, outgoing, and fun to be around. But he couldn't stand Dave's constant complaining. Instead of truly being engaged in the conversation, Kevin said "mm-hmm" a lot and rarely provided feedback. He dreaded their calls but didn't think it would be nice to say anything or try to change the pattern of their communication.

Kevin considered himself a relatively assertive, take-charge type of person, but he couldn't fathom hurting his best friend's feelings.

He wanted to preserve their friendship while creating some distance in their interactions. He tried ignoring some of Dave's calls, but when Dave said, "I called you earlier," Kevin felt he had to give a valid reason for not answering his phone. Since he didn't have a valid reason, however, he continued answering.

"What can I do, without feeling guilty about not picking up his calls?" Kevin asked me. Immediately, we began talking about ways to respond and how to manage his discomfort. I told him that even though easing his discomfort wouldn't happen overnight, the more he practiced setting a boundary, the more assured he would feel.

Initially, I asked Kevin to start talking more about himself to see if that would shift the dialogue. He noticed that helped some, but Dave still complained most of the time. Then I asked Kevin to steer the conversation by saying, "Tell me something good that happened today." That strategy helped as well, but Dave still complained. Kevin decided he could handle talking to Dave once a week for fifteen minutes instead of their usual thirty minutes.

For the most part, Kevin stuck to what we discussed. When he didn't, however, he immediately suffered the consequences of a draining dialogue for thirty minutes twice a week.

Set a Boundary or Suffer the Consequences of Not Setting One

Outside of family, friendships are the hardest relationships in which to implement boundaries. Your friends are often open with you about who offended them and how they felt. This makes it very difficult to set a boundary if you believe it's the exact thing they're likely to perceive as mean or offensive. But there is hope, and many friendships have survived these requests. Perhaps your friends will as well. And remember, if a relationship ends because of a boundary, it's a sign of a bigger problem. According to my Instagram Stories polls, 81 percent of people have had an issue with the way friends talk about their dating habits. When problems are not addressed and boundaries are not set, relationship challenges persist.

Our relationships are a reflection of our boundaries or lack thereof. Other people have no idea of our listening capacity or emotional capacity, so it's up to us to use our words and behaviors to make them aware.

How do we exercise our boundaries guilt-free? Again, we can't. But they are like muscles. The more we set them, the easier they become to set and maintain. We assume our friends will be heartbroken if we set a boundary. This is probably because we hear them complain about how others treat them. But is it possible they might be responsible for some of the issues they have with others?

I had a friend in college who complained about the things her boyfriend and other friends said about her. For a while, I listened, but then I started to evaluate the truth of these statements about her. It wasn't my job to tell my friend she was wrong, but I also didn't have to listen to her whine about how others had wronged her. It wasn't necessarily "nice" of me to pretend to listen to her while saying "mm-hmm" repeatedly, so I started to shift the conversations toward other topics. To be present, it was vital for me to connect with her on subjects that created an engaging dialogue between us. I liked many things about her and didn't want to end our relationship, so steering our discussions in a different direction allowed me to create a healthier friendship with her.

How do you know the difference between a healthy and an unhealthy friendship?

Signs of a Healthy Friendship
- Your friend wants to see you grow.
- The friendship is mutually supportive.
- The friendship is mutually beneficial.
- Your friendship evolves as you evolve.

- You understand how to support each other.
- Setting boundaries doesn't threaten the friendship.
- Your friend is happy for you to be yourself.
- Your friend acknowledges your quirks and works around them.
- You can talk to your friend about your feelings.

Signs of an Unhealthy Friendship
- The relationship is competitive.
- You exhibit your worst behavior when you're with your friend.
- You feel emotionally drained after connecting with your friend.
- Your friend tries to embarrass you in front of others.
- You don't have anything in common.
- Your friend shares details of your personal life with others.
- The friendship is not reciprocal (i.e., you give more than you receive).
- You're unable to work through disagreements.
- Your friend doesn't respect your boundaries.
- The relationship is enmeshed/codependent.

Dealing with Complaining

Complaining falls into one of three categories: venting, problem-solving, or ruminating. Venting is a way to talk about issues without seeking guidance but to simply let out your frustrations. Problem-solving is seeking guidance or advice on how to correct an issue. Ruminating is talking about the same issues over and over without trying to problem-solve or work through your frustrations in any real way.

Ruminating is essentially dumping on others. Rarely do I hear people have an issue with venting or problem-solving. It's rumination that becomes an issue.

Almost everyone complains about something, but the frequency matters. No one enjoys hearing someone ruminate about the same thing repeatedly. The friend who complains all the time does so without limitation because we have provided a space for it.

Ways to Deal with a Chronic Complainer
1. Empathize when appropriate.
2. Redirect the conversation by changing the subject.
3. Be intentional in your dialogue, and stay on topic.
4. Lead by example; don't complain.
5. Ask before offering an opinion, and be mindful of whether the person can handle the truth.
6. Don't be dismissive (e.g., "It isn't so bad" or "You'll get over it").
7. After you've done all you can, draw a clear boundary around the time allotted for the conversation and how often you will talk.

What to Say to Someone When You Don't Want to Give Them Advice
1. "I'm not sure how to help you with that."
2. "That sounds like a big issue. Have you thought about talking it over with this person who is bothering you?"
3. "How have you thought about handling the situation?"
4. "What I would do is completely biased and based on me. I'd like to explore what you could do in this situation."

If you are the person complaining, it's also helpful to set some boundaries with yourself.

How to Manage Chronic Complaining
1. Pay attention to how often you complain.
2. State whether you're simply venting or looking for feedback.

3. Consciously consider the purpose of your conversations with people.
4. Work through feelings by journaling, which is beneficial.

Reasons Behind Boundary Issues in Friendships

The older we become, the harder it is to create new friendships and renegotiate old ones. It particularly becomes harder to make friends after we reach thirty. As we grow older, our ability to nurture and give time to our friendships competes with parenting, work, romance, and family relationships.

After thirty, people often experience internal shifts in how they approach friendships. Self-discovery gives way to self-knowledge, so you become pickier about the people you surround yourself with, according to Marla Paul, author of the book *The Friendship Crisis: Finding, Making, and Keeping Friends When You're Not a Kid Anymore.* "The bar is higher than when we were younger and were willing to meet almost anyone for a margarita," she says.

We tend to overthink the interactions more. "Will they like me?" or "Did I say the right thing?"

When we maintain a friendship for ten years or more, we become accustomed to specific roles in the relationship. Therefore, shifting our boundaries seems like a betrayal of the relationship. But people change all the time. As we grow in friendships, other areas of our lives likely grow as well.

With my friends from high school, we've had to learn to adjust as we transitioned to college, our first "real" jobs, serious dating relationships, and perhaps marriage and children. All life changes require a shift in boundaries, and some relationships don't survive the changes. The dismissal is perhaps an indication of a crack in the foundation of the relationship, not the result of the new request. As we change, it's simply natural for some friendships to fall away.

Common Boundary Issues in Friendships

Being the Relationship Adviser

I once had a friend who insisted on sharing her relationship issues with me. I kindly asked her not to share the ins and outs of her relationship with me because it was making me feel jaded toward her boyfriend. Initially, she didn't understand. But after my consistent redirection, she got the point.

Setting this boundary didn't ruin our friendship. Our relationship would have suffered if I had continued to listen and shared my honest feedback. It wouldn't have been healthy for either of us.

Nothing requires you to be the dating expert for your friends. You can listen, share stories, and help them problem-solve. But if doing any of those things makes you feel uncomfortable, you can shift gears.

Loaning Money and Possessions

"My friend always wants to borrow money. How should I handle this?"

Possible Boundaries

1. Set your expectation up front: "I will loan you ____ with the expectation that you'll pay it back by ____. If, for any reason, you can't meet my deadline, give me a heads-up at least the day before."
2. "I'm not able to loan you any money."
3. "I'm not able to give you ____, but I can offer ____."

Keep in mind that when you loan money and possessions, you're making yourself a lending source for others. If you don't want to be a lending source, stop offering your resources.

Offering Unsolicited Advice and Feedback
"I don't like my friend's wife. What should I do?"

Possible Boundary
Learn to coexist peacefully. Your friend won't leave his partner just because you don't like her. Telling him will likely cause an unnecessary rift, because it's an issue that can't be resolved.

Getting Burned Out from Advice-Giving
"My friend is always dating the same kind of person. I've told her over and over that she needs to date a different type."

Possible Boundaries
1. You've told her what you think, and she isn't listening. Stop repeating yourself.
2. Bite your tongue when your opinion isn't valued.
3. Allow people to make their own mistakes and experience their own outcomes.

Receiving Unsolicited Advice and Feedback
"My friend is always telling me what to do with my life. How do I make them stop?"

Possible Boundaries
1. Stop inviting them in. Share less. Your friends respond to what you tell them.
2. Say, "I need you to listen to me. I don't want any advice or feedback." Tell them that you want to vent without being given any advice or comments.

Dealing with a Needy Friend

"My friend constantly wants me to do things with them, and it's excruciating."

Possible Boundaries

1. Stop agreeing to show up in a way that you can't maintain long-term.
2. Allow for healthy distance in your friendship with time together and apart.
3. Decide which things you enjoy doing with this friend, and do only what you enjoy with them.

You Are Not a Therapist—You're a Friend

Unfortunately, in friendships, there's often an expectation that we can talk about all things. This expectation sets many of us up for disappointment, because no one knows everything about every topic. Instead, friends offer 100 percent biased advice based on their own experience.

In some cases, it's fine to tell people what you would do if you were in their situation. But when a friend is ruminating or stuck on a particular issue, the best thing you can do is refer your friend to an expert.

Times that you may want to refer someone to a therapist include the following:

- Your friend seems stuck on a specific issue, talking about it over and over.
- Your friend discusses unresolved trauma.
- Your friend is experiencing prolonged grief.
- Your friend is a danger to themselves or others.
- You notice symptoms of depression, anxiety, or other mental health issues.

- Your friend is talking about their relationship, and you feel inept at helping.

When people need therapy but come to you instead, do this:
- Remember that you are a friend, not a therapist in your relationships.
- Offer them resources to get started, such as books or contact information for therapists or support groups.
- Once you have given them the resources, set boundaries around how much and how often you will allow them to vent to you.
- Let them know that you've assisted them in the ways that you believe to be most helpful.
- Encourage them to seek help by emphasizing that you are not equipped to help them appropriately.
- Ask if they followed through on the resources you suggested.

Whether your friend needs therapy, a mechanic, a nurse, etc., leave the expertise to the experts.

Enmeshment Does Not Make You a Good Friend
In high school, I was given the book *The Value in the Valley*, by Iyanla Vanzant. In her chapter titled "The Valley of O.P.P. (Other People's Problems)," Vanzant notes:

> We are not indebted to anyone in this life. We are accountable to some, responsible for others. We are never, however, obligated to take the weight of another's life on our shoulders.

Reading those words in high school was quite helpful, but in college, when I began to separate myself from other people's problems, it felt like a huge weight was lifted off my chest.

For years, I, too, believed that being a "good friend" meant dealing with my friends' problems as if they were my own. It's important to realize that your friends' issues are not your issues. Overly entangling yourself in other people's problems is not an indicator of how much you love them. Instead, it shows your lack of healthy boundaries.

You can be there for people without entangling yourself in their feelings, solutions, and outcomes. The most loving thing you can do is listen. The most empowering thing you can do is allow people to work through their own problems. When you find yourself ruminating about someone else's issues, stop and remind yourself that the issues aren't yours. Tune in to your feelings and why you might be stuck on someone else's problems. Enmeshment is a distraction from real ways that we can help others and be there for them. You have never helped anyone by worrying about them and thinking endlessly about their problems.

Dealing with Chronic Boundary Violators

As I've said, people will do what you allow, and they will do it over and over again until you stop them. It's true that you can't control what people do to you, but you can manage your reaction and what you tolerate.

Being healthy will require you to
- Eliminate toxic people from your life
- Minimize the frequency of your interactions with unhealthy people
- Do things alone rather than with unhealthy people

- Make hard choices about how you choose to spend your time
- Try something different because the same approach yields the same results
- Set clear expectations at the beginning of a new friendship
- Build new relationships with healthy people
- Repeat your boundaries more than once (or move on because people are unwilling/unable to honor yours)

Sometimes, we have to end unhealthy relationships because the other person refuses to accept our boundaries. It's never easy to leave a relationship, even when it's unhealthy or no longer fits who we are. We often stay stuck in relationships because we hyperfocus on returning the friendship to how it used to be. But if we have changed, the relationship may no longer be appropriate for the person we've become.

It's hard to determine the best time to end a relationship, and the truth is that there is no "best" time. Of course, there are poorly chosen times, such as after a huge life event. But perfect timing may never come.

These things may need to happen before you leave an unhealthy relationship:
- You may need to give up trying to think of ways to fix something that can't be fixed.
- You may need to get tired of talking to your friends about the same problems.
- You may need to get tired of having values that you aren't honoring.
- You may need to ask for what you want, see it happen temporarily, and notice that the changes are short-lived.

- You may need to figure out how to exist without this person in your life.
- You may need to realize that the bad outweighs the good.
- You may need to be honest with yourself about how the relationship is impacting your wellness.

———————————————————————❋———————————————————————

Friendships are ended in the following ways:

1. Ghosting, which is vanishing from the relationship with no explanation, not answering calls, and ignoring all attempts to connect. Some people feel most comfortable with this form of passive communication if the other person is likely to allow them to walk away quietly without confrontation.
2. Not quite recovering from a massive blowup but keeping the friendship alive on life support. Basically, it's sort of over, but there's some occasional interaction.
3. Allowing things to fizzle out quietly. This method is preferred by many because nothing has to be said or done. It's an amicable agreement to take time and space away from the relationship.
4. Having a conversation to air out frustrations and verbalize openly that the relationship is over.

You know your friends. You know which friends can handle a closing conversation and which ones can't. Choose the method that's best for you and the other person.

Exercise

Grab your journal or a separate sheet of paper to complete the following exercise.

❋ Describe your idea of a healthy friendship.

❋ Identify with whom you have healthy friendships.

❋ List your unhealthy friendships and define what makes them unhealthy.

❋ Determine what needs to be said or done to improve the friendship.

13

Work

People treat you according to your boundaries.

Janine loved her job, but she hated her work environment. Sammie, one of her coworkers, came to her cubicle every day to gossip about everyone in the office. Even though she didn't like it, she sometimes participated because she didn't want to seem rude.

Then Sammie started asking Janine to go out for drinks after work, but she didn't want to go. Every time she was asked, she'd say something like "I can't tonight. I already have plans after work."

But since Janine wasn't clearly saying no, Sammie kept asking. And because Janine seemed engaged in the office gossip, Sammie kept gossiping.

Janine dreaded seeing Sammie, but she felt it would be mean to say anything. Sammie caused her to be distracted at the office, which even caused her to have to take work home. Outside of her issues with Sammie, Janine often helped her coworkers with their assignments and took on additional projects from her boss. She considered her work environment toxic because she felt overworked and was frustrated by the office gossip.

After twelve years at that job, Janine thought her only solution was to start looking for a new job. But before you leave a job or relationship, it's always important to first consider these questions:

"Have I tried setting any boundaries?"

"In what ways do I contribute to this situation?"

"What can I do to make this situation healthier?"

Instead of standing in her power to control her boundaries at work, Janine thought starting fresh somewhere else would alleviate her issues. But she was bound to take her unhealthy boundaries with her to any workplace. The fresh start she needed was with herself.

Set On-the-Job Boundaries

At work, as in the rest of life, it isn't realistic to try to get your needs met through waiting for situations to improve magically. Bouncing from one unhealthy circumstance to the next won't help either. You can't outrun your inability to set boundaries. So Janine would need to implement them wherever she worked. If I had to guess, she would have similar, if not worse, boundary issues elsewhere.

Janine struggled deeply with the need to be liked—not just by certain people, but by everyone. She would bend herself to fit and do whatever kept her in the good graces of others. So if that meant being inauthentic, she tolerated that discomfort. As a people-pleaser, she feared setting limits.

She worried that she would sound aggressive if she said "Get away from my desk" or "I'm not helping you with anything." And yes, those are aggressive and mean ways to set boundaries. Instead, she could be assertive instead of aggressive, by saying things such as

"Let's chat during lunch. I have a few projects I need to push through."

"I have a lot of things on my plate, so I can't help you with your project."

In chatting with Janine, we reviewed all the areas about her job that caused her frustration and resentment. Then we compiled the following list:

Boundaries for Janine
1. Say no to requests for assistance from coworkers.
2. Stop participating in office gossip.
3. When office gossip is brought up, make a clear statement about disinterest.
4. Say no to requests for after-work gatherings (when she genuinely doesn't want to attend).
5. Before agreeing to new projects from her boss, allow others to work on it when possible and/or delegate the tasks to others.

Janine came to realize that she wasn't in a toxic work environment. She just hadn't been setting appropriate boundaries.

Everyday-Boundary Issues at Work

The Office (the U.S. version) is one of my favorite TV shows. I began watching this show while in grad school, and at that time I was just becoming acquainted with the idea of boundaries.

In the show, Michael Scott is the boss of a small paper company who suffers from constant unhealthy boundaries and self-centeredness. Michael's boundaries are so unhealthy, in fact, that his employees are always trying to reel him in and caution him about appropriate workplace behavior. He's unaware of the needs of the others around him and how his conduct has impacted them.

In one of my favorite episodes, "Diversity Day," Human Resources holds a training to teach Michael about proper workplace etiquette. In true Michael Scott fashion, he hijacks the training by doing an inappropriate Chris Rock skit and makes a word-association game out of racial terms, Black history figures, and religions. The funny part of this show is that Michael is so oblivious about the offensiveness of his behavior. He has no clue that he's crossing boundaries. Isn't this typically the case? The person violating limits has no idea how they're affecting others.

Boundary issues at work look like
- Doing work for others
- Being asked about personal issues
- Taking on more than you can handle
- Not delegating
- Flirting
- Working without pay
- Not taking advantage of vacation days
- Saying yes to tasks you can't responsibly complete
- Engaging in stressful interactions
- Working during downtime
- Doing jobs intended for more than one person
- Not taking needed time off

Sure, some people may be aware when they violate someone's boundaries, but most likely, they don't know. Boundaries are not common sense; they're taught. In the workplace, they're passed down by the HR department, the work culture, and the bosses. When people are in fear of losing their jobs, however, it's hard to implement boundaries.

Boundaries are not common sense; they're taught.

IN 2017, WOMEN began coming forward about sexual assault at the hands of the media giant Harvey Weinstein. He has allegedly assaulted at least eighty women, and for many years they didn't come forward for fear of being blackballed in Hollywood. Given his power and influence, he was able to continue with inappropriate workplace boundaries. (He has denied all allegations.)

According to the *New York Times* article "Harvey Weinstein Paid Off Sexual Harassment Accusers for Decades," he created a toxic work environment in which he sexually harassed, assaulted, and bullied women in the workplace for three decades. His poor behavior was allowed because it was the culture, and he was labeled "an old dinosaur."

Even if your boundaries are dismissed because of "the culture," it doesn't mean they aren't relevant and vital. It might mean that you need to tell others in the company, seek support outside the organization, or get legal advice. It isn't okay to feel like your job will be in jeopardy if you don't comply with toxic workplace behavior.

Handling a Toxic Work Environment

In a toxic work environment, your emotional and mental health status is put in jeopardy. When your work environment is truly toxic, your ability to function at home or in personal relationships will be affected.

A toxic environment might include
- Working long hours
- Gossiping by several people
- Not being paid for additional work
- Cliques among coworkers

- Being mandated to complete more work in a limited time frame
- Negative communication among peers or superiors
- A narcissistic boss
- Being bullied
- Being sexually harassed
- Being mistreated based on race, physical ability, or sexual orientation

---

A toxic work environment is devoid of healthy boundaries, but before deciding the situation can't be improved, it usually makes sense to try setting some. Then, be consistent to see if the changes take hold long-term.

It's also important to remember that you don't have to join in the toxicity. If you're in a toxic work environment, try this:

1. Consider which boundaries might be the most helpful.
2. Identify healthy people in the toxic environment.
3. Document, document, document your issues with dates and times.
4. If your boss isn't part of the problem, talk to your boss.
5. Speak up about your needs in meetings, to superiors, and with coworkers.
6. Talk to Human Resources about the office culture.
7. Find support outside the office to manage your work-related stress, such as talking to a therapist.

Burnout and the Impact on Work-Life Balance

Burnout is a response to unhealthy boundaries. Many of the clients I see in my practice report issues with work-life balance. For fourteen years, I've observed people doing the work of two people, not leaving work on time, working after hours (evenings and weekends), not using allocated vacation time, and volunteering for projects they don't have time to do. They do this all in the name of being a "good employee."

I have cautioned them, "The more you appear to handle, the more work you'll be expected to handle."

One of the things I hear most is, "I know you're burned out because you listen to people talk about their problems all day." When I tell people, especially other therapists, "I'm *not* burned out from my work as a therapist," they're surprised. Is it unbelievable to think that a person who talks about boundaries all the time could actually have some pretty decent ones?

Here is a list of things I do to limit the possibility of burnout:
- I have a cap of fifteen to twenty clients per week.
- I have three days dedicated to seeing clients, and the other two days I write or work on other projects.
- I see clients only within my niche (relationship issues).
- Before taking on new clients, I speak to them to see if we align energetically.
- I share my boundaries with my clients about how to contact me after hours.
- On the days I see clients, I'm intentional about managing my energy, such as avoiding potentially draining conversations outside work.
- I spend a few minutes before my first session in quiet, while I consider the day and set the tone.
- I recognize that I don't have to be a therapist outside of work hours, so I don't counsel people off the clock.
- I see a therapist myself to process issues as they come up in my life.
- I go on several vacations throughout the year.

Here are some other ways to avoid burnout:

- Don't allow one day of vacation time to go unused. Vacations are an opportunity to recharge and reset. Take advantage of this when you have an employer that offers paid time off. If your employer doesn't offer time off, save up (if you can), and take some time to recharge. Getting out of the workplace is a meaningful way to restore your energy.
- Make time for yourself outside work. Find a hobby that has nothing to do with your job, and take part in it regularly.
- Take your lunch break away from your desk. If you must sit at your desk, don't work through lunch. Take this time to meditate, watch an episode of *The Office*, go for a walk, or have lunch with a coworker while chatting about non-work-related things.
- Prioritize time for yourself either before or after work. Before you start your workday, take a few minutes to engage in a relaxing practice such as meditating for a few minutes, reading something uplifting, or watching something motivational. Taking a few moments before, throughout the day, or after work, will help you center your thoughts, lower your blood pressure, and provide some balance.

How to Set Boundaries at Work

1. Identify the areas where boundaries are needed. You can uncover these by tuning in to your feelings. What's causing you to stay later? What about your job leads you to feel overwhelmed or burned out? One of my first jobs out of college was as a juvenile probation officer/case manager. Social workers have a notoriously high rate of burnout, and my office was no different. With large caseloads, daily crises, and high demands, the organization was an essential place to have boundaries.

Knowing how the job could be unpredictable, I proactively completed whatever I could in advance, such as treatment plans and court reports. Doing this saved me a lot of frustration when I found myself in the middle of a crisis on a deadline day. I learned to get organized because I got fed up with the frustration of being disorganized. It helped that while at this full-time job, I was a full-time grad school student going to classes or an internship in the evening. If I wanted to keep my job, I had to set clear boundaries so I'd be able to leave on time.

2. If at all possible, do your work only at work/only during work hours.

3. Give yourself permission to have boundaries at work. Just because you're at work doesn't mean you can't set limits. Holding back about what you need will create resentment toward your coworkers and employer.

4. Don't let issues go too far before you decide to set boundaries. Start setting them right at the onset of possible issues.

5. Teach others how to respect your boundaries by being consistent with respecting them yourself. If you choose to declare your expectations, be clear and up front.

Boundaries at work sound like
- "I won't be able to take on any additional projects."
- "I cannot work past five o'clock."
- "I don't check work emails while on vacation."
- "I need more assistance with my workload."
- "I don't talk about personal subjects at work. It makes me uncomfortable."
- "If you want to chat, let's have lunch together; that way, I can focus on our conversation."
- "Thank you for inviting me to hang out with you this weekend, but I won't be able to make it."

- "I don't want to grab drinks after work, but how about going to a yoga class?"
- "I'm not available to help you with your request after hours. I like to focus my time on my family."
  - In the case of work, it's okay to provide details about why you're saying no, such as "I won't be able to assist on this project because I'm helping ____ on their project."

Boundaries in the office look like
- Trying *not to* eat lunch at your desk, but if you do, don't work while eating lunch
- Being direct about ending conversations that distract you from working
- Arriving at work on time
- Leaving work on time
- Minimizing distractions such as texting and calls to family and friends during the workday, as these exchanges prevent you from finishing your work on time
- Taking a nap on your lunch break; studies show that taking naps improves willpower and focus
- Closing your office door to minimize distractions
- Figuring out strategies to avoid taking work home, if possible

---

How to Set Boundaries Away from the Office
- Use all your allotted vacation days. According to the U.S. Travel Association, in 2018, American workers failed to use 768 million days of paid time off—a 9 percent increase from 2017.
- Don't check work emails on the weekend.
- Don't go into the office to catch up on the weekend.
- Don't work while on vacation unless it's an emergency. Plan for coverage, and delegate all you can while you're away.

- Find hobbies and activities that have nothing to do with work.
- If your job is stressful, limit the way you talk about it with others, unless it's your therapist. Ruminating about all the things you hate will not improve your feelings.
- Don't offer your professional services for free to friends and family. If you're an accountant, for example, refer your friends and family to another accountant.
- Set an out-of-office email and voicemail response when you're on vacation. Direct the caller to another person to reduce the number of issues you'll have to address when you return.
- Delegate tasks that someone else can do. CEOs should never answer their own phones. Doctors shouldn't prepare their operating rooms for surgeries.
- Prioritize tasks in order of urgency and deadline. Everything at work doesn't merit the same level of importance.
- Minimize distractions such as chatting with coworkers if it throws you off course.
- Ask for assistance when you need it.
- Inform your employer when your workload is too heavy.

Boundaries for Entrepreneurs

- Charge your full fee.
- If you offer a reduced rate, do so sparingly.
- Don't work all the time. Take breaks. Pause. As a fellow entrepreneur, I know that you consistently have work to do, but guess what? You're the boss, and you can define your limits.
- Avoid using phrases that are about working nonstop, such as "hustle harder," "on the grind," and "rest later."

How to Communicate Boundaries to Your Boss

People base your ability to perform on what they think is reasonable for your role, on the needs of the company where you work, and sometimes on what your boss sees themselves as capable of doing. For instance, if a boss works in the evening and while on vacation, they may expect you to do the same. Doing anything different might be frowned upon.

When this is the case, it's your job to advocate for reasonable expectations, not requirements based on your boss's lack of boundaries. Of course, you would never say "You're unreasonable because you have unhealthy boundaries." Instead, you might say, "It's important to me to recharge when I'm out of the office in order to be fully present when I'm at work. I'd like to restrict my work, as much as possible, to the following time frames."

When communicating your needs to your boss, be sure to use "I" language. Make it about you, not them.

Don't say this:
"You always give me things to do when you know my plate is full." If you say this, your boss might feel attacked and will be less likely to consider your request.

Instead, say this:
"I work best with deadlines. As you give me an assignment, I will prioritize your request, but if something is urgent, please let me know."

If your boss refuses to acknowledge healthy boundaries, bring others into the situation. Reach out to Human Resources if the issue can't be resolved with your boss.

Saying No to Social Invitations and Out-of-the-Office Connections

Most of us spend around thirty-five to forty hours a week working. In the office, you may build some healthy connections and eventually establish some friendships. But what happens when you don't want to hang out after work or go to lunch with your coworkers or boss?

Setting boundaries might look like

- Not hanging out with particular coworkers after work
- Not offering to help your boss with personal things
- Allowing a coworker to follow you on social media but restricting what they can view
- Muting a coworker whose content you don't enjoy
- Not giving your coworker your social media handle

Saying no to invites sounds like

"Thanks for inviting me to your holiday party, but I won't be able to make it."

"It's kind of you to invite me to lunch, but I'd like to spend time alone during lunch."

"After work, I like to go home and relax."

"How about we exchange phone numbers instead of social media handles?"

"I'm a homebody, so I'm not interested."

Overcoming the Fear of Perfection

There is no such thing as the perfect employee. You can have ethical boundaries and still be a good employee, coworker, or entrepreneur. In every workplace, there's a person who has at least one boundary that everyone values about them. In this case, copy what you see.

If you happen to have a boss with poor limits, you don't have to mimic their issues. Be very clear about yours, and if they're challenged, speak up immediately.

It's true that setting boundaries will sometimes upset others. Consider this: work is where people spend the majority of their time, and your time is valuable. Therefore, being comfortable in the space where you spend the most time is essential for your well-being.

Exercise

Grab your journal or a separate sheet of paper to complete the following exercise.

* What is one boundary that you can implement in any work environment?
* What is your work schedule?
* What times are you willing to work outside of your work schedule?
* Given what you know about your boss, what's the best way to set boundaries with them?
* Do you need to set any with your coworkers?
* How do you think you'll benefit from setting boundaries at work?

14

Social Media and Technology

Self-discipline is the act of creating boundaries for yourself.

Tiffany's partner, Lacey, was attached to her phone. She carried her phone with her from room to room, even spending about an hour in the bathroom with it. Whenever Tiffany asked Lacey what she was doing, she would answer through the door, "I'm using the bathroom!"

Tiffany was convinced that Lacey's phone usage was preventing them from connecting with each other. As full-time students who didn't live together, their time was limited. That time was even more limited since Lacey spent a significant portion of it staring at that little screen. Even when they hung out with friends, Lacey continually checked her phone.

In my sessions with Tiffany, she described her relationship with Lacey as a stressor. She loved her girlfriend, but she hated the way Lacey always seemed preoccupied. They had never directly talked about the phone usage, however. Tiffany just assumed that Lacey should know better, but as we discussed, maybe Lacey didn't "know better."

We discussed ways that Tiffany could directly address the issue in their relationship. It seemed best that she start by making requests such as "While we're watching this movie, I'd like you to put your phone down," or "Put your phone down so we can hold hands." Once Tiffany asked, she was surprised by how easily Lacey complied.

Lacey probably had no clue that her phone usage impacted her ability to connect with her partner. She was simply distracting herself during moments that she felt were downtime.

People often complain that technology gets in the way of their relationships. Throughout this chapter, I will use the term "technology" to describe time spent online, with social media, watching TV, or playing video games.

In no way, of course, is technology inherently bad. But sometimes people use it in an excessive or harmful manner, or they use it as an escape or distraction. When we feel uncomfortable, it's become commonplace to distract ourselves by grabbing our device.

I have personally had to learn how to manage my time on technology. In June 2019, I was featured in an article in the *New York Times* called "Instagram Therapists Are the New Instagram Poets." From there, my popularity on Instagram increased significantly.

It started in 2017, when I began to post intentional content geared toward mental and emotional wellness, highlighting the benefits of therapy and addressing relationship issues. From January 2019 to July 2019, I went from having two thousand followers to having one hundred thousand followers. The weirdest thing about my growth on social media was that I barely used it at all before 2017, personally or professionally. I had Facebook from 2009 to 2010, and I had a personal Instagram account. But I rarely posted, and I followed only a small number of accounts. Until I started my professional Instagram account, @nedratawwab, I didn't have a daily experience with social media.

For many years, I felt the joy of missing out (JOMO) on social media. Being out of the loop had plenty of advantages. For one, I enjoyed it when people told me their interpretations of what was happening in the world according to social media. Also, I didn't have to deal with the awkwardness that came along with following certain friends, coworkers, or family members but not others. Even now, as a person who regularly engages on social media, I cater my social media experience to fit what I want. For example, if I'm trying to save money, I don't follow fashion influencers who inspire me to shop. If I'm interested in vegan meals, I follow a few of those accounts.

Going from rarely using social media to being an influencer has been quite a journey. In many ways, I enjoy it, but there are times when I, too, experience the downsides, such as managing the time I spend. I also have to deal with negative comments and manage the expectations of my community.

Things I'm Reminded of When Posting on Social Media

- There is always someone out there whose standards you aren't meeting.
- People are much harsher when they think you won't respond.
- Some people like to argue.
- Once you start responding to them, you agree to partake in an argument.
- What people say about you is based on them, not you.
- You can't please everyone, because everyone's needs are different.
- Explaining yourself over and over doesn't mean people will eventually get it.
- Sometimes you have to release people by using the power of the block feature.
- It's your job to protect your energy.
- Some people feel entitled to your time, but your time is yours to manage.

Because we exist in a digital world, technology is a massive part of how we function. Even with technology all around us, we can curate a healthy digital experience.

Here are some signs that you might need boundaries with your digital usage:
- You find yourself constantly checking your phone when you're supposed to focus on something else.
- You spend excessive amounts of time on your phone. The average person spends about three hours a day on their phone.
- In social settings, you're glued to your phone instead of socializing.
- You regularly use your phone as an escape from working, parenting, completing tasks, or being present with others.
- People have complained about your digital usage.
- You use your phone while driving.
- Your technology usage impacts your ability to function in other areas, such as in school, at work, or at home.
- Your technology usage hurts your mental or emotional health.

How to Manage Information Overload in the Digital Age

As a therapist, I've often heard people talk about the downsides of social media: feeling left out, comparing themselves with others, and the pressure to fake it. I was worried about getting sucked in. I also feared contributing in a way that made others feel less than or jealous. But what I've learned is that you can't control the way people respond to what you share.

Sure, as a therapist, I post with intention, and I try to consider how my posts might be perceived. Nevertheless, someone, somewhere, often finds a way to view my message in a way that wasn't intended. I've learned that their interpretation has little to do with me and everything to do with what's going on in their own life.

To a large degree, our digital consumption is within our control. When we don't like what we see, we have a choice to continue looking/watching or to move on to something else. The moment we continue to follow something that bothers us, we agree to be bothered.

Managing Bad News When It's All Over TV and the Internet

You are who you follow, what you watch, and the websites you visit. You have the power to choose your user experience. In moments when something substantial happens in the world, you can remove yourself from the sources that drain your energy. If being informed comes at the cost of your sanity, make a temporary choice to minimize your digital usage.

Boundary Suggestions for Managing Your Intake of Bad News

- Turn off the news alerts on your phone.
- Designate a specific time of day to watch or listen to the news intentionally.
- Unfollow people who continuously post about tragedies or topics that impact your mood.
- Kindly tell people when you don't want to hear about specific news stories.
- When significant events happen in the world, it's okay to spend time temporarily away from the internet, TV, and social media.
- Head over to your favorite streaming service, and start a new TV series.

Ultimately, make peace with being out of the loop sometimes, not seeing every meme, and not being able to recite every detail of what happened. Stepping away may spark the fear of missing out (FOMO), but it can serve as a useful way to engage in other areas of your life. Once you're feeling better, or when the news has subsided, feel free to rejoin the digital landscape.

Following Friends, Family, and Associates

Following people on social media has become a great way to stay in contact. Today, people often exchange Instagram handles instead of phone numbers. But once you start following someone, how do you stop? The more people you follow, the more you learn about who they are and how they want to present themselves to others. If you like what they represent, it's wonderful to share that with them. But when you find out your favorite coworker has the messiest relationship *ever* with her boyfriend, all highlighted in her posts, it's hard to unsee what you didn't want to know. And it's hard to unfollow someone you see often in real life.

Common Complaints

"I hate following my friend because she pretends to be someone she's not."

"My sister posts too many pictures of her kids."

"I'm so annoyed by my boss's political commentary, but I'm afraid to unfollow him."

Solution

People can be whatever version of themselves they want online. You can't control this, but you can control whether you follow them. If you don't feel comfortable unfollowing someone, mute them or hide their profile if that's an option.

Boundary Suggestions for Engaging with People You Know

- Make it hard for people to follow you by creating a private account.

- Follow people, but hide their content if you don't feel comfortable unfriending or blocking them.
- Opt to exchange phone numbers instead of social media handles.
- Follow people whose content you genuinely enjoy.

As an active social media user, I've enlisted a particular set of boundaries that I regularly post and keep in my highlights on my Instagram page. I'm not suggesting that everyone needs to write a set of boundaries. Still, I think it's something to consider if you're using a social media account for professional purposes, if you're an influencer, or if you receive a lot of requests. Openly discussing yours is a way to outline instructions for your community.

My Instagram Boundaries
1. I am a licensed therapist. I *do not* provide therapy via DM. I do not offer personal opinions about life decisions such as "Should I dump my boyfriend?" Those are your decisions to make. I do not confirm or deny if you're right or wrong in your decision-making.
2. I am generous in creating content. I appreciate requests for specific types of posts. However, I create based on inspiration, the needs of my community, and my expertise.
3. I receive a lot of requests to help people find a therapist. I do not know therapists in every city, state, and country. Refer to Google or your insurance provider/Employee Assistance Program/ community outreach center to find a therapist in your area.
4. You are free to repost my content. *Always* give credit where credit is due.
5. I honor myself (and others in my community) by deleting comments and blocking people who are judgmental, mean-spirited, or demeaning.

6. If you are my client, you *can* follow me. Ethically, I cannot engage (i.e., follow or respond to DMs from my clients).
7. If you have questions, please ask them on Mondays during my Q&A.
8. Keep in mind that I'm human. I cannot respond to every comment or DM, but I try to read as many as possible.
9. If you are experiencing a mental health crisis, call 911, or find a therapist near you.

Even with clear boundaries in place, people attempt to test them. It's my job to uphold mine by sticking to what I've outlined.

Common Boundary Issues with Technology
Spending Too Much Time Watching Television
These days, TV is with you wherever you go. You can view your favorite show on your tablet or phone, as well as your TV at home. My personal preference is watching on my iPad. It's portable and convenient. But television consumption becomes an issue when you're distracted from getting things done or when it hinders your ability to engage in other areas of your life.

For example, maybe you stay up late, night after night, watching TV and face the consequences of sleep deprivation the next day.

Spending Too Much Time on Social Media
According to a *Washington Post* article, 3.725 billion people use social media. That's half the world's population. The average adult spends about 142 minutes a day on social media. The average teen spends about nine hours a day on social media. How much time do you spend? I know nearly three hours sounds like a lot, but when you consider how many people passively browse social media sites while waiting to meet with a friend or while standing in line, the minutes

add up. Of course, this usage becomes an issue only when you're using social media at times you're supposed to be doing something else.

For example, let's say you have to be at work at 8:00 a.m. You wake up at 7:00 a.m., knowing it takes you fifteen minutes to get to work, but you lie in bed for forty-five minutes browsing social media. As a result, you wind up late to work. At this point, the usage is impacting your obligation to be at work on time.

As a therapist, I know that appropriateness depends on a lot of other life factors. If you're a parent with a young child at home, for example, it might be hard to appropriately spend five hours a day on social media while parenting your children. However, if you're single with no kids, and it's a Saturday, perhaps spending five hours on social media doesn't impact other areas of your life. I would wonder, however, what other things you could be doing with your time, what are you getting from your constant online connection, and what the meaning behind your consumption is. Ultimately, *why* we use social media is as important as *how much* we use social media.

Nir Eyal's book *Indistractable: How to Control Your Attention and Choose Your Life* offers a view of how social media and devices are not the issue. Instead, people are the issue, as they create problems with social media and technology use. It's important to understand the *why* behind your usage. Is it intentional? Is it a reflex? Is it problematic?

Boundaries to Consider

If You Can't Get Out of Bed Without Grabbing Your Phone

Don't sleep with your phone near your bed.

Place your phone so far away from your bed that you have to walk across the room to grab it.

Don't sleep with your phone in your room.

Instead of grabbing your phone, consider other ways you'd like to spend the first moments of your day, such as journaling, cuddling with your partner, stretching, or brushing your teeth. Find something else to do.

If You Regularly Check Your Phone

Keep your phone out of reach. Put it on the charger in another room. Practice turning it off for a few hours a day. Intentionally plan times to engage on social media, and decide on times when social media is off-limits.

If You Spend Excessive Amounts of Time on Social Media

Track your usage. iPhones allow you to set a social media time limit, and once you reach your limit, you will be logged out of all social media apps or prompted if you want to override the limit. Within some apps, you can set an alert reminding you about the amount of time you've spent on social media. Respect your boundaries by honoring the time constraints you've set for yourself.

If You Experience Low Self-Esteem, Low Self-Worth, Envy, or Resentment

In my Instagram Stories poll, 33 percent of respondents said that they find it hard to unfollow people when they are upset or not interested in the other person's content.

Be mindful of who you follow and why. Even if all your friends are following a famous influencer, you can choose not to follow that person if you find that you envy their lifestyle and feel worse about your own. Unfollow, block, and mute people who make you feel uncomfortable. Your reaction may indeed be something you need to work through, but work on yourself and revisit those accounts later.

Adults Unable to Put Down Devices

A friend of mine told me her young son asked, "Do you love your phone more than me?" She was hurt, but so was he. Devices are like a laptop in our hands. We can watch TV, listen to podcasts, shop, socialize, and so much more. But at what cost?

Are you grocery shopping on your phone while your kids try to tell you about their day? Are you socializing with your online friends while having dinner with your real-life friends? You need parameters.

Boundary Questions

1. What are some times that might be inappropriate to use your phone?
2. How can you practice being present with others?
3. Is it okay to not always be available to others via phone?

Kids Using Devices

Kids will inevitably use devices, but adults are responsible for creating boundaries around how devices can and should be used.

Possible Boundaries

- Do not allow devices at dinnertime.
- Do not allow while doing homework unless it's being used for the assignment.
- Do not allow devices after a specific time on nights and weekends.
- Incorporate movement breaks in between time spent on devices.
- Use parental-control apps.
- Monitor social media usage.
- Remove televisions from kids' bedrooms.
- Model appropriate device usage for children.

- Watch along with your kids, and talk to them about the content they're viewing.
- Talk to them about proper usage versus inappropriate usage.

Fear of Missing Out (FOMO)

FOMO is real. People care so much about staying in the loop that they spend endless amounts of time trying to stay relevant and connected with the "in" crowd. It costs money, time, and energy to always be in the loop. Unfortunately, with social media, people are constantly bombarded with images, sound bites, and videos of other people doing well and appearing to have fun. Rarely do people consider the amount of time it might take an influencer to post the perfect picture.

Lala Milan, an Instagram influencer with more than three million followers, says it took her six hours to record and edit a sixty-second video. Companies are even starting to create social media photo experiences to appeal to people who crave the perfect photo opportunity.

Social media gives people attention in ways that were unimaginable before its invention. The worst thing is seeing your friends, exes, and associates doing fun things without you. As a result of feeling left out, people question who they are or their importance in the lives of others. If you struggle with FOMO, consider who you follow. If it's people you don't know, think about the impact that following them has had on your mental health. If it's people you know, don't allow your ego to get in the way. Let them know you'd like to be included in their next adventure. Invite them to do something with you. But also realize that their social life separate from you is no reflection on their relationship with you.

Infidelity as a Result of Inappropriate Online Interactions

Since half the world's population has a social media account, that includes your crushes, exes, and new people waiting to be discovered. If you're single, enjoy it. If you're in a relationship, create some boundaries about technology usage. When couples haven't communicated their boundaries, unspoken ones are guaranteed to be violated.

Social Media Boundary Questions for Couples

- Is it okay in your relationship to follow exes or people you've had a sexual relationship with in the past?
- How should you address DMs from people who seem romantically interested?
- Should you friend/follow each other on social media?
- Are there any expectations about posting pictures of each other?
- Is it okay to talk about relationship issues online or on social media?
- What's your philosophy on liking sexually suggestive photos?
- Are there individual accounts you'd rather your partner not follow?

Discussing your boundaries prevents common issues that can threaten your relationship.

Strategies to Minimize Digital Overload

Social Media Cleanse

There are two ways to do a digital cleanse.

Option #1

Restrict yourself completely from using social media by removing yourself from it for a certain amount of time. Many people find it helpful to remove social media apps from their phones as a way to make it harder to take a look.

Option #2
Reduce your engagement.

Limit the number of accounts you follow on social media. Set a goal, for instance, and cut the number of people you follow by half.

Use a timer, and stick to the limit you set.

Use social media only during designated times.

Remove the apps from your phone, and use social media only when you're on your computer.

TECHNOLOGY IS A part of our lives, and our dependence on it will grow. But you're in charge of how you engage with it. Technology isn't the problem. Social media isn't the problem. Human engagement and consumption are more significant issues. You conquer technology when you find ways to use it to your benefit. Responsible usage requires implementing boundaries as to how you use it.

Additional tips:

- Limit your access by not keeping multiple chargers in multiple spaces.
- Let your phone die. Use the time while it's charging to recharge yourself.
- Use the screen-time feature on your phone to monitor your usage.
- Erase nonessential apps. Any app not used in the last month isn't essential.
- Turn off notifications. Alerts trigger you to pick up your phone.

- Create rules about phone usage. Start big, and decrease weekly until you're comfortable with the amount of time you spend on your phone.
- Unfriend people who aren't real friends.
- Unfollow people who make you feel bad about yourself.

Exercise

Grab your journal or a separate sheet of paper to complete the following exercise.

* How many hours do you spend using technology?
* How many hours would you like to spend using technology?
* In what areas of social media and gaming would you like to limit your usage?
* When you find yourself mindlessly using technology, what do you feel?
* What healthy habits would you like to implement instead of consuming technology?

15

Now What?

Your wellness hinges on your boundaries.

The first time I went to therapy was in grad school. Like most people, I showed up to therapy with issues such as relationship problems, anxiety, and work-life-balance issues. I had no clue what to call the issues in my relationships with others. All I knew was that people were always trying to make me feel bad, guilt-tripping me for setting boundaries such as "I can't loan you money anymore," "When you borrow my car, put gas in it," or "I can't babysit for you because I have class." I was constantly frustrated and resentful because the people in my life were always asking for something and never willing to show up for me.

After several sessions, my therapist gently told me to grab a copy of *Boundaries: Where You End and I Begin* by Anne Katherine. With the help of the therapist and the book, I started to feel better about saying no and asking for what I needed.

Depending on whom I'm asking, I still sometimes feel odd when making a request. But I do it anyway, because ultimately I feel better when I have healthy boundaries in my relationships. I'd rather deal with the discomfort in the short term than resentment and frustration in the long term.

In healthy relationships, it's okay, rational, and safe to state your boundaries. It goes both ways, however. You can have them, and the other party may also have them. For example, your boss may have a boundary that you show up five minutes early to meetings, and you may have one that you don't work on weekends. Respecting other people's limits is a beautiful way to leverage respect for your own.

When someone implements a new boundary with you, such as "I would like you to put your phone away while we're having dinner," the best way to respond is by affirming and upholding the request. Verbally, your response could be "I understand. I will put my phone away." Then ensure that your phone is put away.

After reading this book, you know that when someone implements a boundary, it's to help them feel safe, happy, and secure in the relationship. These limits aren't to be taken personally. The second (and my personal favorite) agreement from the book *The Four Agreements: A Practical Guide to Personal Freedom*, by Don Miguel Ruiz, is "Do not take anything personally." So whatever happens around you, don't take it personally. Nothing other people do is because of you. It's because of themselves. All people live in their own dream and their own mind. Even when words seem personal, such as a direct insult, they really have nothing to do with you.

I constantly work with my clients to depersonalize events and interactions with others. When we personalize, we negate the personal story and history of the other people involved. Personalizing assumes that everything is about us.

I'm the sort of person, for example, who prefers that people take their shoes off in my house. I believe what we carry on our shoes shouldn't be brought indoors, and it means less mopping for me. In the early days of my rule, several people questioned my practice. "Why do I have to take *my* shoes off?" But my rule isn't about them. It certainly wasn't a comment on their choice of footwear.

The same is true of your boundaries and the people who ask you to honor theirs. Without questioning someone, you can agree to the request or suffer the consequences of not accepting it. But remember, you can't determine your consequences. If your boundary is in direct conflict with someone else's, it's essential to evaluate which is healthy and will be most helpful for the relationship. Remember, rigid boundaries are not healthy.

Boundaries are established in two parts: (1) verbally communicating them to others, and (2) taking action, whether implementing consequences or removing yourself from interactions with people who won't or don't respect your boundaries.

After you've done all you can, the ultimate boundary might be to end an unhealthy relationship. This is an unfortunate but sometimes unavoidable circumstance. When you choose to end a relationship because it's no longer viable, remember that you tried. In your effort to repair the relationship, you offered solutions that could have worked. It's possible that if the situation changes, you can make up with the other person.

Here are a few tips to consider when rekindling relationships:
- What do you expect to be different?
- Has the situation/person truly changed?
- What is the evidence that the person/situation is different?
- Are you well matched with the other person, or are you merely fixated on the relationship working out?
- If nothing has changed, are you willing to repeat what you experienced before?

Hoping a relationship will improve without assessing it realistically will land you back in a similar or worse situation than before.

At first, setting your boundaries may be uncomfortable. You might feel riddled with guilt. You might question if you're doing the right thing. But set them anyway. Push past the discomfort, and do it even while you feel afraid. You're challenging yourself to be healthier and to have healthier relationships.

Ambivalence is a part of the process, and it's perfectly natural to feel insecure while trying something new. Then, once you start setting boundaries, stay the course, because consistency is the most crucial part of the process.

Remember: there is no such thing as guilt-free boundary setting. If you want to minimize (not eliminate) guilt, change the way you think about the process. Stop thinking about boundaries as mean or wrong; start to believe that they're a nonnegotiable part of healthy relationships, as well as a self-care and wellness practice.

Creating healthy boundaries is how you ensure that you're happy and well in your relationships and in life. For them to stay implemented, be clear about them verbally and through your actions. Remember that when someone doesn't agree with or understand your boundaries, they may push back, question, test your limits, ignore, or ghost you. No matter what, don't stop setting them. Persevere with the awareness that your boundaries are not for people to like. They're for you to remain healthy in your relationships. They're a way for you to set ground rules for yourself and others. And they're useful in all areas of life: technology, work, your relationship with yourself, and your relationships with others. So it's okay to have boundaries and to communicate them assertively. Only with boundaries can you peacefully coexist with others.

Situations, relationships, and people struggle to survive without boundaries. Here are just a few of the benefits:

- People with boundaries sleep better.
- People with boundaries experience less burnout.
- People with boundaries have healthier relationships that tend to last longer.
- People with boundaries experience less stress.

- People with boundaries feel more joyful.
- People with boundaries benefit from the short- and long-term value of setting them.

Thank you so much for your willingness to be brave and to change. I promise that the journey toward healthier boundaries is worth the discomfort of setting them.

Set your boundaries, knowing that you are improving your life, not harming others.

Self-Assessment Quiz

1. "I say yes to a person when I want to say no."

A. Yes, I do that often.

B. I say no and tell people why I'm saying no so that they don't ask me anymore.

C. I usually say no without apologizing or lying about it.

2. "I feel like I'm constantly having to save people close to me and fix their problems."

A. No, I don't get involved in other people's issues.

B. Yes, often.

C. No, I know my limitations and offer what I can, when I can.

3. "I regularly find myself sucked into pointless fighting or debating."

A. Yes.

B. No, I don't experience that.

C. No, I try to keep people at a distance.

4. "I loan money to friends or family out of feelings of pity, guilt, obligation, or being threatened."

A. Yes.

B. No, I loan money with clear expectations of when I'd like to be paid back.

C. No, I don't trust people and/or I want to hold on to every penny I earn.

5. "I frequently feel stressed about work."

A. Yes.

B. No, I never think about work. When I'm off, I check out and don't care what happens.

C. No, I turn off work notifications and ignore calls, texts, or emails. I try to be present with my friends/family/self once I'm home. There are some situations when I might be a little flexible (in case of emergencies or during a big project), but I make sure I don't get sucked into it for too long.

6. "I think I spend too much time on social media."

A. Yes.

B. No, I enjoy checking in on social media once in a while but don't get lost in it.

C. I log on to my social media account for work on specific days and times. Then I log out of the app on my phone.

7. "I feel guilty when I say no to someone."

A. Yes.

B. No.

C. No, I don't care what people think. I'm annoyed/angry/frustrated when they ask me for things.

8. "I get roped into activities or obligations that I don't want to do."

A. Yes.

B. No.

C. No, people know not to ask me to do things.

9. "I don't trust people."

A. True.

B. Not true of all people.

C. No, I trust everyone, and sometimes that causes problems for me.

10. "I share too much personal information too soon."

A. Yes.

B. No.

C. I don't trust people enough to share personal information.

11. "I'm able to hear no from people and not take it personally."

A. Yes.

B. No, I tend to take it personally.

C. I don't usually ask people for help. I don't think they'll do it right, or I can't trust them.

12. "I fail to speak up when I'm treated badly."

A. True.

B. No, I cut people off, I cuss people out, or I gossip about them.

C. No, I'm able to tell people how I feel.

13. "I feel guilty for dedicating time to myself."

A. No, I know I need to take care of myself in order to take care of others. "You can't pour from an empty cup."

B. Yes.

C. No, I prioritize my own needs over everyone else's.

14. "I apologize for things when they're not my fault."

A. No, things aren't typically my fault.

B. Yes.

C. No, I apologize when I've done something I'm responsible for and know I've hurt someone.

15. "I feel scattered and stressed because I have a million things to do and not enough time."

A. Yes.

B. Honestly, I don't have a lot going on. Life is quiet because I don't have a lot of friends or commitments.

C. No, I've learned to say no, outsource, delegate, or ask for help to avoid feeling scattered or stressed.

16. "I don't speak up when I have something important to share."

A. Yes.

B. No, I know that my ideas and input are just as important as everyone else's.

C. No, in fact, I find myself silencing others at work or not giving them a chance to speak up.

Answer Key

See which type of boundaries show up for you the most.

1. A. Porous, B. Rigid, C. Healthy
2. A. Rigid, B. Porous, C. Healthy
3. A. Porous, B. Healthy, C. Rigid
4. A. Porous, B. Healthy, C. Rigid
5. A. Porous, B. Rigid, C. Healthy
6. A. Porous, B. Healthy, C. Rigid
7. A. Porous, B. Healthy, C. Rigid
8. A. Porous, B. Healthy, C. Rigid
9. A. Rigid, B. Healthy, C. Porous
10. A. Porous, B. Healthy, C. Rigid
11. A. Healthy, B. Porous, C. Rigid
12. A. Porous, B. Rigid, C. Healthy
13. A. Healthy, B. Porous, C. Rigid
14. A. Rigid, B. Porous, C. Healthy
15. A. Porous, B. Rigid, C. Healthy
16. A. Porous, B. Healthy, C. Rigid

Created by Nedra Tawwab and Kym Ventola

Commonly Asked Questions

What's a good boundary for a toxic mother that you aren't ready to cut off?
When you're aware that a relationship is unhealthy but you aren't ready to leave that relationship, you can maintain self-boundaries around how you choose to engage with the other person.

Boundary suggestions:

- Consider speaking to your mother less often. Instead of daily, try a few times a week or once a week.
- Limit the length of the conversations. An easy way to do this could be creating a hard out, such as talking to your mother on the way to an appointment. You'll have to end the call when you arrive at your destination.
- Respond when you're ready and willing to talk, not every single time your mother calls or texts.

Is it necessary to explain to a friend or family member why you're creating distance or that you want to cut them off?
You know your people best. Some will listen while you explain, and some will attack you or defend themselves. Be mindful of the type of

person you're addressing before deciding to talk about issues. If the situation is likely to become volatile, it may not be in your best interest to speak to the person face-to-face. Perhaps sharing your desires via text is best. When possible, try to slowly distance yourself from them, as this is often the most cordial way to leave a relationship.

How can I deal with my friend who always complains about work?
You could set boundaries as to how often you talk to your friend about certain topics. It's extremely important to consider how you might be inadvertently inviting your friend to talk more about their issues.

Consider this:

1. Do you seem interested in the topic? For example, bringing up work might give the impression that you want to hear about the topic.
2. Do you offer your friend advice?
3. Have you tried redirecting your friend to a different subject?
4. Have you ever suggested that your friend speak to a professional or higher-up at work about the concerns?
5. Is your friend aware that you find the conversations emotionally draining? If not, change the conversation to a lighter topic.

How can I be a support to a friend who won't go to therapy?
You can decide how much you will listen to and how you're able to help your friend. Choose to remain in your role as a friend, not a therapist. Let your friend know that there are specific topics you don't feel comfortable addressing. Continue to suggest therapy to your friend, and let them know why you think they'll benefit. Some people have deep wounds that friends cannot help them resolve.

How do I explain that I can't loan my family any more money?
When you explain your boundaries, people are allowed to refute them.

Just say,

"No."

"I'm not able to help you."

"Perhaps, I can help you with some resources."

"I can't help; have you explored other options?"

How do I set boundaries with my son without hurting his feelings?
Someone set boundaries with you, and you're okay. Set yours, knowing that you are doing it with love. Boundaries provide structure for your child.

How do I stop feeling guilty?
Change the narrative from "Everything is my fault" to "I am not responsible for everything that happens." Ridding yourself of guilt is saying you want to rid yourself of emotions. You have had to deal with all emotions, including jealousy, happiness, and guilt. The more you focus on the guilt and try to stop it, the longer it will linger. Just feel. Don't judge what you feel.

Acknowledgments

Before I knew what boundaries were, I developed mental limitations around things I thought were inappropriate or things that didn't feel right. Eventually, I learned the word for those limitations was "boundaries." Through a series of small, brave acts, I started the work of setting and keeping boundaries. I'm deeply grateful for the process and the unfolding of the power of healthy boundaries.

Thank you to God for revealing to me why my life has unfolded the way it has, giving me life experiences that would allow me to live as my highest self, and for helping me form my life into words for others to receive. Thank you to my husband for listening to my vision for this book, dreaming with me, and for encouraging me to take the time to focus on writing. Thank you to my two daughters, who revealed to me the boundaries needed to be a parent. Thank you to my sister-friend Erica for our deep conversations about boundaries and for pushing me to be more of myself. Thank you to my Morning Mastermind crew—Racheal, Rebecca, and Monica—for being my cheerleading squad. I have so many wonderful friends—Talaya, Delesa, and others—who throughout this process wrote me beautiful cards, sent me gifts, and made me laugh; thank you. Thank you to all my clients who revealed my passion for helping people create boundaries. Thank you to my community on Instagram for encouraging me to create, always supporting my content, and helping me take my work to new heights. Every single day, I'm privileged to do something I love and help others.

Thank you, Laura Lee Mattingly (my agent), for helping me navigate the publishing world and for pushing me (quickly) through writing a proposal. This project was made easy because Marian Lizzi (my editor) believed in this work from the very beginning and her thoughtfulness about conveying my message helped me shape this book. Thanks to her team, Jess Morphew (art director), and Rachel Ayotte (editorial assistant) for guiding me through this process. My attorney, Patrice Perkins, helped me consider the many aspects of my brand. And my assistant, Shaunsie Reed, cheered me on and reviewed my first draft. This book came to fruition because of the helpers I've found along the way.

I am grateful for the support of my therapist, who encouraged me to write this book and highlighted my triumphs of being boundaried.

Thank you, Mom and Dad, for delivering me into the world. And the biggest THANK YOU is to everyone who read this book. You are brave and you are boundaried.

Further Reading

Allan, Patrick. "How to Deal with Chronic Complainers." *Lifehacker*,
October 8, 2019. https://lifehacker.com/how-to-deal-with-chronic
-complainers-1668185689.

Beck, Julie. "How Friendships Change in Adulthood." *The Atlantic*, October
22, 2015. https://www.theatlantic.com/health/archive/2015/10/how
-friendships-change-over-time-in-adulthood/411466/.

Bourne, Edward. *Anxiety and Phobia Workbook*, 4th ed. Oakland, CA: New
Harbinger Publications, 2006.

Charles Schwab. *Modern Wealth Survey*. May 2019. https://content.schwab
.com/web/retail/public/about-schwab/Charles-Schwab-2019-Modern
-Wealth-Survey-findings-0519-9JBP.pdf.

Clear, James. *Atomic Habits*. New York: Avery Publications, 2018.

Coleman, Jackie, and John Coleman. "The Upside of Downtime." *Harvard
Business Review*, December 6, 2012. https://hbr.org/2012/12/the-upside
-of-downtime.

Derald Wing Sue, "Microaggressions: More Than Just Race," *Psychology
Today*, November 17, 2010. https://www.psychologytoday.com/us/blog
/microaggressions-in-everyday-life/201011/microaggressions-more-just-race.

Emery, Lea Rose. "The First Year of Marriage Is Tough, No Matter How You
Spin It." *Brides*, November 2019. https://www.brides.com/story/the-first
-year-of-marriage-is-tough.

Eyal, Nir. *Indistractable: How to Control Your Attention and Choose Your
Life*. Dallas: Ben Bella Books, 2019.

Higgs, Michaela. "Go Ahead and Complain. It Might Be Good for You."
New York Times, January 9, 2020. https://www.nytimes.com/2020/01/06
/smarter-living/how-to-complain-.html.

Horsman, Jenny. *But I'm Not a Therapist: Furthering Discussion About Literacy Work with Survivors of Trauma*. Toronto: Canadian Congress for Learning Opportunities for Women, 1997. https://eric.ed.gov/?id=ED461078

June, Sophia. "Instagram Therapists Are the New Instagram Poets." *New York Times*, June 19, 2019. https://www.nytimes.com/2019/06/26/style/instagram-therapists.html.

Kantor, Jodi, and Megan Twohey. "Harvey Weinstein Paid Off Sexual Harassment Accusers for Decades." *New York Times*, October 5, 2017. https://www.nytimes.com/2017/10/05/us/harvey-weinstein-harassment-allegations.html.

Katherine, Anne. *Where You End and I Begin—How to Recognize and Set Healthy Boundaries*. Center City, MN: Hazelden, 1994.

Mechling, L. "How to End a Friendship." *New York Times*, June 14, 2019. https://www.nytimes.com/2019/06/14/opinion/sunday/how-to-end-a-friendship.html.

Milchan, A., S. Reuther, J. F. Lawton, G. Marshall, R. Gere, J. Roberts, R. Bellamy et al. *Pretty Woman*. Buena Vista Pictures, 1990.

Morrish, E. "Reflections on the Women, Violence, and Adult Education Project." *Focus on Basics 5*, issue C, February 2002. http://www.gse.harvard.edu/~ncsall/fob/2002/morrish.html.

Rosenwasser, Penny. "Tool for Transformation: Cooperative Inquiry as a Process for Healing from Internalized Oppression." *Adult Education Research Conference*, pp. 392–396. Vancouver: University of British Columbia, 2000. http://www.edst.educ.ubc.ca/aerc/2000/rosenwasserp1-web.htm.

Tawwab, Nedra. "The Question I'm Asked Most as a Therapist—and My Answer." Shine, November 2019. https://advice.shinetext.com/articles/the-question-im-asked-most-as-a-therapist-and-my-answer/.

"Trauma Affects Trust in the World as a Beneficial Place, the Meaningfulness of Life, and Self-Worth." Horsman 1997; Morrish 2002; Rosenwasser 2000.

Tsukayama, H. "Teens Spend Nearly Nine Hours Every Day Consuming Media." *Washington Post*, November 5, 2015. https://www.washingtonpost.com/news/the-switch/wp/2015/11/03/teens-spend-nearly-nine-hours-every-day-consuming-media/.

Vanzant, Iyanla. *The Value in the Valley: A Black Woman's Guide Through Life's Dilemmas*. New York: Fireside, 1995.

Webb, Jonice. *Running on Empty*. New York: Morgan James, 2012.

Williams, A. "Why Is It Hard to Make Friends Over 30?" *New York Times*, July 13, 2012. https://wwwn.nytimes.com/2012/07/15/fashion/the-challenge-of-making-friends-as-an-adult.html.

Notes

Chapter 2: The Cost of Not Having Healthy Boundaries

29. **An article published by the *Harvard Gazette*:** A. Powell, "Study: Doctor Burnout Costs Health Care System $4.6 Billion a Year," *Gazette*, July 19, 2019, https://news.harvard.edu/gazette/story/2019/07/doctor-burnout-costs-health-care-system-4-6-billion-a-year-harvard-study-says/.

30. **According to Emily Nagoski and Amelia Nagoski:** Emily Nagoski and Amelia Nagoski, *Burnout: The Secret to Unlocking the Stress Cycle* (New York: Ballantine Books, 2019).

35. **According to the Anxiety and Depression Association of America:** Anxiety and Depression Association of America, "Facts and Statistics," https://adaa.org/about-adaa/press-room/facts-statistics.

46. **"What's on Your Plate?":** "What's on Your Plate?" was created by Monica Marie Jones and modified by Nedra Tawwab.

Chapter 3: Why Don't We Have Healthy Boundaries?

55. **At Barnes & Noble in 2018, books about self-care outsold books on diet and exercise:** M. Schaub, "Mental Health Books Outsell Diet and Exercise Books at Barnes & Noble," *Los Angeles Times*, January 11, 2019, https://www.latimes.com/books/la-et-jc-mental-heath-book-sales-20190111-story.html.

Chapter 7: Blurred Lines: Make It Plain

122. **According to Kate Kenfield, a sex and relationship educator:** Kate McCombs, "My Favorite Question Anyone Asks Me When I'm Having a Rough Day," blog post, December 3, 2014, http://www.katemccombs.com/favoritequestion/.

123. **According to Celeste Headlee:** Celeste Headlee, *We Need to Talk* (New York: Harper Wave, 2017).

132. **In *Atomic Habits,* James Clear talks about the importance of making small changes to generate significant results:** James Clear, *Atomic Habits* (New York: Avery, 2018).

Chapter 8: Trauma and Boundaries

140. **common boundary violations that often occur when trauma is experienced:** Claudia Black, *Repeat After Me* (Las Vegas: Central Recovery Press, 2018).

Chapter 9: What Are You Doing to Honor Your Boundaries?

151. **the average American carries a credit card balance of $8,398 and has at least four credit cards:** Bill Fye, "Key Figures Behind America's Consumer Debt," Debt.org, https://www.debt.org/faqs/americans-in-debt/.

151. **59 percent of Americans live paycheck to paycheck:** Charles Schwab, *Modern Wealth Survey*, May 2019, https://content.schwab.com/web /retail/public/about-schwab/Charles-Schwab-2019-Modern-Wealth -Survey-findings-0519-9JBP.pdf.

158. **According to the *Journal of Marriage and Family Studies*:** Perspectives Counseling. https://perspectivesoftroy.com/men-cheat-women/.

Chapter 10: Family

177. **In the book *Babyproofing Your Marriage*:** Stacie Cockrell, Cathy O'Neill, and Julia Stone, *Babyproofing Your Marriage: How to Laugh More and Argue Less as Your Family Grows* (New York: William Morrow Paperbacks, 2008).

Chapter 11: Romantic Relationships

201. **Fundamental identities may shift from wife to mother or from lovers to parents:** Matthew D. Johnson, "Have Children? Here's How Kids Ruin Your Romantic Relationship," *The Conversation*, May 6, 2016, https://theconversation.com/have-children-heres-how-kids-ruin-your -romantic-relationship-57944.

Chapter 12: Friendships

210. **Self-discovery gives way to self-knowledge:** Marla Paul, *The Friendship Crisis: Finding, Making, and Keeping Friends When You're Not a Kid Anymore* (New York: Rodale Books, 2005).

214. **In high school, I was given the book *The Value in the Valley*:** Iyanla Vanzant, *The Value in the Valley: A Black Woman's Guide Through Life's Dilemmas* (New York: Fireside, 1995).

Chapter 13: Work

223. **In 2017, women began coming forward about sexual assault at the hands of the media giant Harvey Weinstein:** Jodi Kantor and Megan Twohey, "Harvey Weinstein Paid Off Sexual Harassment Accusers for Decades," *New York Times*, October 5, 2017, https://www.nytimes .com/2017/10/05/us/harvey-weinstein-harassment-allegations.html.

228. **Taking a nap on your lunch break:** Jackie Coleman and John Coleman, "The Upside of Downtime," *Harvard Business Review*, December 6, 2012, https://hbr.org/2012/12/the-upside-of-downtime.

228. **in 2018, American workers failed to use 768 million days of paid time off:** U.S. Travel Association, https://www.ustravel.org.

Chapter 14: Social Media and Technology

234. **In June 2019, I was featured in an article in the *New York Times*:** Sophia June, "Instagram Therapists Are the New Instagram Poets," *New York Times*, June 19, 2019, https://www.nytimes.com/2019/06/26/style /instagram-therapists.html.

236. **You spend excessive amounts of time on your phone:** "How Much Time Do We Really Spend on Our Smartphones?," Straight Talk, September 15, 2018, https://blog.straighttalk.com/average-time-spent-on-phones/

240. **According to a *Washington Post* article, 3.725 billion people use social media:** H. Tsukayama, "Teens Spend Nearly Nine Hours Every Day Consuming Media," *Washington Post*, November 5, 2015, https://www .washingtonpost.com/news/the-switch/wp/2015/11/03/teens-spend -nearly-nine-hours-every-day-consuming-media/.

241. **Nir Eyal's book *Indistractable: How to Control Your Attention and Choose Your Life* offers a view of how social media and devices are not the issue:** Nir Eyal, *Indistractable: How to Control Your Attention and Choose Your Life* (Dallas: Ben Bella Books, 2019).

Chapter 15: Now What?

250. **The second (and my personal favorite) agreement from the book *The Four Agreements*:** Don Miguel Ruiz, *The Four Agreements: A Practical Guide to Personal Freedom* (San Rafael, CA: Amber-Allen Publishing, 1997).

Index

Note: Page numbers in parentheses indicate intermittent references.

About the Author

Nedra Glover Tawwab is a licensed therapist and sought-after relationship expert. She has practiced relationship therapy for fourteen years and is the founder and owner of the group therapy practice Kaleidoscope Counseling. Every day she helps people create healthy relationships by teaching them how to implement boundaries. Her philosophy is that a lack of boundaries and assertiveness underlies most relationship issues, and her gift is helping people create healthy relationships with themselves and others.

Nedra earned her undergraduate and graduate degree from Wayne State University in Detroit, Michigan. She has additional certifications in working with families and couples, as well as in perinatal mood and anxiety disorders, plus advanced training for counseling adults who've experienced childhood emotional neglect.